This publication is dedicated to the authors, agents, publishers, book distributors, booksellers and librarians who bring us books that enrich our lives.

ACKNOWLEDGMENTS

With more than 75,000 new books being published every year, it's a daunting task to identify "discussible" titles. We all know from experience that there are a lot of good reads out there — far beyond the titles that find their way to Oprah's Book Club or the *New York Times* bestseller list. Limited marketing and advertising budgets often mean that book groups would never find out about suitable choices without a publication like *Reading Group Choices*.

We wish to thank the authors, agents, publicists, and our publishing colleagues who continue to support this publication and bring readers quality books for group discussion:

Algonquin Books of Chapel Hill
Back Bay Books (Little, Brown & Co.)
Bantam Doubleday Dell
Broadway Books
Calliope Press
Curbstone Press
Doubleday Books
Christine Goff
Paul Greenberg
Haven Books
Innisfree Press
Alfred A. Knopf
Orlando Place Press
Penguin Publishing Group
Random House
TOR Books
Vintage Books (Random House)
Wildcat Canyon Press

Authorlink Press
Ballantine Books
Be Who You Are Productions
Susan Butler
Donna Woolfolk Cross
Disc-Us Books
Paul Fitzgerald
Elizabeth Gould
Harcourt
Wil Hazzard
Stephanie Kane
Louisiana State University Press
Pelican Publishing
Picador (St. Martin's Press)
Simon & Schuster
University of Alabama Press
Warner Books

In appreciation of an ongoing alliance with Paz & Associates and their efforts in producing *Reading Group Choices*, we thank **Gena Kennedy** for her cover design, and **Rich Printing Company**.

Group
Choices

Selections for Lively
Book Discussions

Paz & Associates

2002

For further information, contact:
Mark Kaufman, Editor
Reading Group Choices

Paz & Associates
800/260-8605 — phone
mkaufman@pazbookbiz.com — email

Visit our websites at:
www.readinggroupchoices.com
www.pazbookbiz.com

ISBN 0-9644876-7-5

Cover design: Gena Kennedy

Printed by:
Rich Printing Company, Inc.
7131 Centennial Bl.
Nashville, TN 37209
615/350-7300

INTRODUCTION

It should come as no startling revelation that the world has changed, that our lives will never be the same, in the aftermath of September 11th, 2001. We hunger for information to help us make sense of the world around us, and even more so for a sense of connection to our family, friends and neighbors.

What could be more valuable than a book group to help meet these needs? Whether it's the opportunity to learn something new, gain a different perspective, test deeply held beliefs, or simply to enjoy the camaraderie of other book lovers, people are drawn to book groups in greater numbers than ever.

And what better resource than *Reading Group Choices* to facilitate a lively group? Descriptive summaries, endorsements, and topics not only help group members decide what to read (within the group and on their own), but also keep the discussion on track. As was the case with all seven previous editions, this year's collection of titles is noteworthy for its diversity — there is truly something for everyone.

In resonance with the times, there are several stories of personal challenge, such as *Free, Leaving Katya,* and *The Pilot's Wife.* When faced with challenges, it's always nice to have hope, inspiration and faith — so you'll find a few titles with those themes as well, like *Lying Awake.* Triumph over adversity — another timely topic — can be found in titles like *Man and Boy* or *Moving From Fear to Courage.* And, now that the world seems to have become so much smaller, with conflict and struggle ever present, we can learn more about holy warriors in *Afghanistan the End of Illusion* or a world of child warriors in *Shadow of the Hegemon.*

As more of us revisit the question "What matters most?", and find the answer in those we hold dear, several titles in this year's collection, such as *Dale Loves Sophie to Death, Infidelity,* or *An Unfinished Marriage,* help us define love, marriage, and the nature of relationships, as well as the very essence of being.

If you're looking for some good new reads to spark your group's discussions throughout the year, we hope that you will enjoy browsing this collection. You'll find that you will be thinking about the topics long after the discussion has ended. What better proof that books can open minds, broaden horizons, and change lives!

Mark Kaufman and **Donna Paz**

December, 2001

CONTENTS

CONTENTS (continued)

CONTENTS (continued)

AFGHANISTAN:
The End of Illusion
& THE VOICE
(special offer, two book set)

Authors: **Paul Fitzgerald &**
Elizabeth Gould

Publisher: Imprintbooks, 2001

Website: www.grailwerk.com

Available in:
Paperback, 300 pages, $17.00
(ISBN 1-59109-171-3)

Genre: Fiction and Nonfiction/Cultural &
World Issues/Personal Discovery

Summary

As the first American journalists to enter Kabul behind Soviet lines in 1981, Paul Fitzgerald and Elizabeth Gould have spent 20 years researching the Afghan issue and have created a work that not only provides context, but gives "holy war" and the rise of the Taliban special relevance in today's world. *Afghanistan The End of Illusion* offers insight to the roots of America's "Holy War" against the Soviet Union and how that lead to the creation of the Taliban, and ultimately the death of that tiny nation. *The Voice*, commissioned by Oliver Stone as a screenplay in 1992, originated with the authors' true adventures in Afghanistan during Soviet occupation. It grew into an investigation of the esoteric connection between crusaders, mystical holy warriors, the CIA, and their pursuit of the Holy Grail. The authors have seen behind the veil of secrecy and discovered a "truth" behind the movement of history through their Afghan experience. They have lived the mythology and understand its meaning at the dawn of the new millennium.

Recommended by: *Daily Times — Chronicle*

"...vital to everyone's understanding of the new millennium."

Author Biographies

Journalists **Paul Fitzgerald** and **Elizabeth Gould** have produced news segments and documentaries that have appeared on CBS News, ABC Nightline, PBS, and CNN. They have two children and live in Massachusetts. Visit *www.grailwerk.com* for more background information.

Topics to Consider

1) How does the real experience of Afghanistan lead the authors on a spiritual journey through dreams?

2) *Afghanistan: the End of Illusion* is non-fiction while *The Voice* is called fiction. Where do the books intersect?

3) How does Paul, a contemporary Fitzgerald, connect with the Grail Quest of his family going back to their 12th century invasion of Ireland through dreams? What role does the real Afghanistan experience play?

4) In *The Voice*, Paul's employer is trying to penetrate his dreams electronically. What helps Paul resist being overwhelmed by Lord Gilbert's vast technological resources to get what he wants?

5) How does the role of technology change from the beginning to the end of *The Voice?* Do you think technology will enhance or inhibit the free flow of ideas and access to information? Will it make us more or less humane?

6) The interplay of mythology, genealogy, history and current events is carefully woven through *The Voice.* How does the interweaving help to impart the reality of the authors' Afghan experience?

7) In *The Voice*, Rick hired Paul and his wife to cover the war in Afghanistan for his network. Paul holds him responsible for her accidental death during that shoot. How did you feel about what happens to Rick? How does this connect to the authors' real Afghan experience?

8) When Paul understands who the Black Knight from his dreams is, he is transformed. Did Paul's transformation surprise you? What experiences have happened to you that would compare, such as dreams, visions, near-death, out-of-body, remote viewing, psychic? How have they changed your thinking?

9) Throughout *The Voice*, Paul dialogs with many characters, challenging traditional concepts of religion, spirituality, science and ultimately reality itself. Did the dialogs prepare you for the end of the story?

10) How do you define the Grail? Has your definition been altered by reading these two books?

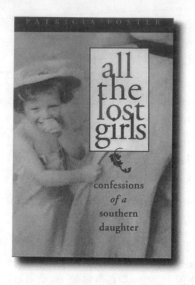

ALL THE LOST GIRLS
Confessions of a Southern Daughter

Author: Patricia Foster

Publisher: The University of Alabama Press, 2001

Website: www.uapress.ua.edu

Available in:
Hardcover, 320 pages. $24.95
(ISBN 0-8173-1047-9)

Genre: Biography/Coming of Age

Summary

Patricia Foster's memoir weaves together the life of a mother and daughter caught in the web of that mother's ambition. The mother, intelligent and driven, but trapped by a heartbreaking secret, is determined that her daughters receive the training that will guarantee their success as professional women. Foster and her sister are brought up as "honorary boys," girls with the ambition of men but the temperament of women, in rural south Alabama in the 1950s and 1960s. Foster's desire is to please her mother, but by the time she reaches age fifteen, her efforts to reconcile the contradictory expectations that she be both ambitious and restrained leave her nervous and needy even as she cultivates the appearance of the model student, sister, and daughter. *All the Lost Girls* charts the difficult unraveling the narrator must do to achieve understanding and autonomy.

Recommended by: Nanci Kincaid, author of *Crossing Blood*

"... I love the way Patricia Foster just wades into that dark and murky love-hate that keeps mothers and daughters forever mysterious to each other."

Author Biography

Patricia Foster is Associate Professor of English at the University of Iowa. She is editor of *Minding the Body: Women Writers on Body and Soul* and *Sister to Sister: Women Write About the Unbreakable Bond* and co-editor of *The Healing Circle*.

Topics to Consider

1) The narrator makes it clear that she lives a middle class life, even with the poverty in her mother's and father's background. What is the legacy of poverty in these characters' lives? How does the residual idea of "class" complicate and illuminate their lives?

2) How does the revelation of mother's terrible secret shape the story? Why do you think the author gave this information at the beginning of the book rather than revealing it in an epiphany?

3) In what ways were the problems of the South different from the problems of the rest of the nation during the 1950s, '60s, and '70s? In what ways were they similar?

4) If American girlhood in the last three decades has been a war between self and image, how does Foster engage in this battle? What does she learn about the divisions in herself? How does this battle affect her sense of identity? Think of your own adolescence and consider how self and image affected your own coming-of-age.

5) Look at the chapter "A Different Kind of Woman." Why is this particular story important to a book about white southern girlhood? What does Foster learn from Ida that she can't learn from the other women in her life?

6) Foster says that she failed to become "a successful middle class girl." What does this failure teach her about herself? About her family? In what ways do you think failure can be a successful teacher?

7) In what ways is the narrator trapped in her mother's concept of ambition? Are there ways in which she defies her mother? Ways in which she concedes? What are the risks of defiance? Discuss the importance of defining a mythology of ambition for oneself.

8) In "Miracle Boys," the narrator's brother defies his father's ambition. What does he seem to gain by this defiance? What does he lose? In what ways does his struggle for selfhood mimic the narrator's struggle for identity? Discuss the significance of gender in affirming an identity in adolescence.

BIG STONE GAP

Author: Adriana Trigiani

Publisher: Ballantine, 2001

Website: www.ballantinebooks.com/
BRC

Available in:
Paperback, 304 pages. $12.95
(ISBN: 0-345-43832-9)

Genre: Fiction/Family/
Personal Discovery

Summary

Nestled in the Blue Ridge Mountains of Virginia, the tiny town of Big Stone Gap is home to some of the most charming eccentrics in the state. Ave Maria Mulligan is the town's self-proclaimed spinster, a thirty-five year old pharmacist with a "mountain girl's body and a flat behind." She lives an amiable life with good friends and lots of hobbies until the fateful day in 1978 when she suddenly discovers that she's not who she always thought she was. Before she can blink, Ave's fielding marriage proposals, fighting off greedy family members, organizing a celebration for visiting celebrities, and planning the trip of a lifetime—a trip that could change her view of the world and her own place in it forever.

Recommended by: *The New York Times Book Review*

"As comforting as a mug of chamomile tea on a rainy Sunday."

Author Biography

Adriana Trigiani grew up in Big Stone Gap, Virginia. She has honed her storytelling abilities over a decade of writing and producing some of television's biggest shows including "The Cosby Show". Trigiani is also an award-winning playwright. She lives in New York City with her husband.

Topics to Consider

1) Why do you think the author set Big Stone Gap during the late 1970s instead of today?

2) As the novel progresses and Ave Maria learns more about herself and her past, her feelings for Big Stone Gap change from contentment to disassociation to joy. Have your feelings for your hometown changed as you've changed? How?

3) When Ave Maria visits Italy she realizes that her home is in Big Stone Gap. Have you had any similar realizations? What makes a place "home"?

4) Theodore and Ave Maria have romantic feelings for each other, but never at the same time. If their feelings had been more coordinated, do you think they would have entered a lasting marriage? Do you think their "best friend" relationship will endure after Ave Maria and Jack Mac's wedding?

5) When did you suspect that Ave Maria would fall in love with Jack Mac? What were the clues that the author left?

6) Jack Mac tells Ave Maria, "Stop thinking." Is Jack Mac correct? Does too much thinking lead Ave Maria into making the wrong choices? Are her emotions a trustier guide or equally unreliable?

7) A common theme in literature is that the heroine must lose a parent or parents before she is free to discover who she really is. Is this merely a literary convention or does it have roots in real life? Does it apply to male characters as well?

8) How much of Ave Maria's personality was shaped by nature and how much by nurture?

9) Do you think Ave Maria's expectations of love and marriage would have been affected if she had learned the truth about Mario before her mother died? How?

10) **Big Cherry Holler**, Adriana Trigiani's next novel about the people of Big Stone Gap, jumps forward eight years into Ave Maria and Jack Mac's marriage. Knowing these two characters as you do, do you expect the path of true to love run smooth for them?

THE BLIND ASSASSIN

Author: Margaret Atwood

Publisher: Anchor Books, 2001

Website: www.vintagebooks.com/read

Available in:
Paperback, 544 pages. $14.00
(ISBN 0-385-72095-5)

Genre: Fiction/Literature/
Family/Intrigue

Summary

This Booker Prize-winning novel opens with these simple, resonant words: "Ten days after the war ended, my sister Laura drove a car off a bridge." They are spoken by Iris, whose terse account of her sister's death in 1945 is followed by an inquest report proclaiming the death accidental. But just as the reader expects to settle into Laura's story, Atwood introduces a novel-within-a-novel. Entitled *The Blind Assassin*, it is a science fiction story told by two unnamed lovers who meet in dingy back street rooms. When we return to Iris, it is through a 1947 newspaper article announcing the discovery of a sailboat carrying the dead body of her husband, a distinguished industrialist. Brilliantly weaving together such seemingly disparate elements, Atwood creates a world of astonishing vision and unforgettable impact.

Recommended by: *Newsday*

"The first great novel of the new millennium."

Author Biography

Margaret Atwood is the author of more than twenty-five books, including fiction, poetry, and essays. Her most recent works include the bestselling novels *Alias Grace* and *The Robber Bride* and the collections *Wilderness Tips* and *Good Bones and Simple Murders*. She lives in Toronto, Canada.

Topics to Consider

1) Laura and Iris spend their childhood in Avilion, "a merchant's palace," and, like princesses in a fairy tale, are virtually untouched by the outside world. What other elements reinforce the fairy-tale-like quality of their lives? What role does Alex Thomas play within this context? Does Iris's depiction of her life as an old woman also draw on the conventions of fairy tales?

2) How was Iris's "choice" between classicism and romanticism affected by the distinctions Iris and Laura's parents made between the two girls when they were children? What incidents show that Iris has ambiguous feelings about the roles she and Laura assume as children? What signs are there that Iris has a romantic side she keeps hidden from the adults? What cost does this exact?

3) How does the science fiction story constructed by the unnamed lovers mirror the story of the lovers themselves and the circumstances surrounding their affair? In what ways does it parallel events in Iris's life, both as a child and as an adult?

4) Discuss Iris's father's role in arranging her marriage. Was he doing the best he knew how, as Iris writes, or was he motivated by reasons Iris doesn't allow herself to acknowledge?

5) Atwood has said that the form of *The Blind Assassin* was influenced by early twentieth-century collages, in which newspaper excerpts were glued onto canvas and then painted around and over — thus framing two ways of representing reality, each of which contradicted the other but also complemented it. How many "kinds" of writing are in *The Blind Assassin*, washroom graffiti included? What purpose does each form of writing serve?

6) Is Iris purely a pawn in a plan conceived by the men, or does she have reasons of her own for agreeing to marry Richard? In what ways does the marriage fulfill Iris's conception of herself and her approach to life?

7) How do the multiple levels of *The Blind Assassin* interact with one another? Do they unfold in concert, shedding light on one another, or is the relationship among them only apparent at the end of the book? What does the use of this narrative technique reveal about Atwood's methods of storytelling?

BLIND SPOT

Author: Stephanie Kane

Publisher: Bantam Dell, 2000

Website: www.writerkane.com

Available in:
Mass market paperback,
320 pages, $5.99
(ISBN 0-553-58175-9)

Genre: Fiction/Intrigue

Summary

Cold, hard evidence—a prosecutor's dream, a defense attorney's nightmare. A killer is stalking women across Colorado's Front Range and posing their decapitated bodies in the spectacular sandstone formations thrusting up from the ancestral Rockies. Called to defend entrepreneur Aaron Best in the grisly slaying of a millionaire's trophy wife, Jackie Flowers turns FBI profiling on its head and retains as her own expert a maverick shrink who thinks nothing of challenging the Feds' techniques. The only hitch is, the pattern they uncover could free or hang her client.

Recommended by: *The Drood Review of Mystery*

"Kane's work is just as good as the trial mysteries written by Steve Martini ... A fine addition to the fraternity of lawyers writing mystery novels."

Author Biography

Stephanie Kane grew up in Brooklyn, New York. She has practiced law for twenty years, first as a partner in the largest law firm in Colorado and then as a criminal defense attorney. She is also the author of *Quiet Time*. She lives in Denver with her husband, a federal judge.

Special offer: The author will chat online or by telephone with any reading group that selects *Blind Spot*. Interested groups should contact the author at **www.writerkane.com**.

Topics to Consider

1) Jackie Flowers has a learning disability which she takes great pains to conceal. How does her disability give her the upper hand in court? What price does she pay for her deception? The word "dyslexia" never appears in **Blind Spot**. Why do you think the author chose not to use it?

2) To what extent is Jackie's success as a trial lawyer attributable to or in spite of her sex? Do women ever have an advantage over male attorneys in court? What advantages do men have?

3) Jackie is the surrogate mother to Lily, an eight-year-old Chinese orphan adopted by her next-door neighbors. What is the source of Lily's bond with Jackie? Why does the girl refuse to read?

4) The defendant, Aaron Best, inherited his father's company, while his brother Mark, the brains of the operation, remained an employee. What role does sibling rivalry play in the plot?

5) Vincent Bugliosi wrote, "Criminal profiling is a double-edged sword. In **Blind Spot**, it becomes a powerful weapon for the defense." Do you think FBI profiles are effective, or can they do more harm than good? Do "textbook killers" really exist?

6) Jackie's expert witness, psychiatrist Richard Hanna, describes psychopaths as "the kind of men you'd want to sit next to at a dinner party," who succeed in business and "pass" in their social group. Have you met any?

7) **Blind Spot** contradicts many popular assumptions about police procedures and the criminal justice system. How accurate do you think this treatment is?

8) The Hollow Man deposits his victims' bodies in ancient rock formations. What is the psychological significance of these sites? What role does the Medusa myth play in the killer's fantasies?

9) Why does the Hollow Man perceive Lily to be a threat? Do children have better radar than adults?

10) What is each character's "blind spot"?

DALE LOVES SOPHIE TO DEATH

Author: Robb Forman Dew

Publisher: Back Bay Books, 2001

Website: www.twbookmark.com

Available in:
Paperback, 256 pages. $13.95
(ISBN 0-316-89066-9)

Genre: Fiction/
Relationships/Family

Summary

The extraordinary first novel that captured the American Book Award in 1982 and heralded an important new voice in American fiction is now restored to print in a new paperback edition. To mark the publication of Robb Forman Dew's major new novel, *The Evidence Against Her*, Back Bay Books takes pleasure in issuing a new paperback edition of her award-winning first work of fiction. *Dale Loves Sophie to Death* explores themes of familial and romantic bonds as it tells the story of a woman whose husband stays behind in New England while she and their children spend the summer in her Midwestern hometown.

Recommended by: *Washington Post Book Review*

"A novel that profoundly satisfies both the mind and the heart."

Author Biography

Robb Forman Dew is the author of *The Time of Her Life* and *Fortunate Lives*, as well as a memoir, *The Family Heart*. She also was a teacher at Iowa Writer's Workshop and has contributed stories to *Southern Review* and *The New Yorker*, among others.

Topics to Consider

1) Discuss *Dale Loves Sophie to Death* as a portrait of a marriage. Do you consider Dinah and Martin's marriage successful? How does it compare with other marriage portraits in the novel?

2) Why did Dinah, as an adolescent, consider dancing to be "far sexier than sex" (page 185)? Do you agree with her perceptions about dancing?

3) Discuss Dinah's response to the birth of her first child (pp. 174-175). Why was she both embarrassed and enraged?

4) Have you ever had a friend like Isobel? How does Dinah and Isobel's friendship change in the course of the novel?

5) Discuss Dinah's response to Toby's illness. Was she irresponsible in not seeking medical help sooner?

6) The novel offers some very sensual and highly detailed descriptions of food. Discuss the special role that food plays in the Howellses' domesticities.

7) Do you consider Dinah responsible for the death of her father's cat? Discuss the role animals play in the novel.

8) "The events that might astonish them now — the only things that could not be foreseen — were the unpleasant surprises" (page 187). Do you agree that Dinah's fate is sealed? That there can lie in store for her no happy surprises?

9) Why do you think Robb Forman Dew chose the title *Dale Loves Sophie to Death*, particularly in view of the fact that Dale and Sophie are not characters in the book? Do you consider the title appropriate for the novel?

For additional topics, see www.twbookmark.com

DEATH OF A SONGBIRD

Author: **Christine Goff**

Publisher: Berkley, 2001

Website: www.christinegoff.com

Available in:
Paperback, 224 pages, $5.99
(ISBN: 0-425-18044-1)

Genre: Fiction/Intrigue

Summary

Lark Drummond's luxury hotel is packed with hundreds of birding convention-goers. Her employees are driving her crazy. And now her friend and business partner, Esther Mills, has cancelled the hotel's coffee shipment. In need of a respite, Lark agrees to accompany her friend, Rachel Stanhope, on an afternoon birdwatching excursion. But their outing turns ugly when Lark peers through her spotting scope and witnesses Esther's murder. With the help of their birdwatching club, she and Rachel set out to find the killers. But as suspects and motives pile up, it soon becomes clear that what they thought was a robbery gone bad was, in fact, something much more sinister.

Recommended by: Tony Hillerman, *NY Times* Bestselling Author

"One needn't be a bird lover to fall in love with Christine Goff's charming Birdwatcher's Mysteries!"

Author Biography

Christine Goff is the author of the bestselling "Birdwatcher's Mystery" series set in fictitious Elk Park, Colorado. Her first novel, *A Rant of Ravens*, was named a finalist for a Women Writing the West 2001 Willa Award for Best Original Paperback. She is currently at work on book number three, *A Nest in the Ashes*. A former journalist, Goff is a self-proclaimed "backyard birdwatcher" with 161 birds on her list. She lives in the Rocky Mountains of Colorado, near where her novels are set.

Topics to Consider

1) How does Goff set the stage for *Death of a Songbird*? What are some of the incidents or situations that forebode trouble early on?

2) Lark Drummond is the pivotal character/protagonist in *Death of a Songbird* — what is it about her personality and character traits that make her such a likable and successful sleuth? What are some examples of when Lark's big heart almost get her into real trouble? Is she too trusting of people?

3) Which characters didn't you like or not trust? Explain why. Which did you like from beginning to end and why?

4) How does the setting and the Migration Alliance Convention play in integral part in the intrigue?

5) An important component in a successful mystery is keeping the reader guessing. Discuss which character or characters you suspected of the murders and what you thought was the motive. Did your suspicions change?

6) Paradox is often what creates stimulating situations. How does Goff so deftly juxtapose a cozy, friendly setting with macabre events?

7) How important do you think the "likeability quotient" of the sleuth is in the success of a mystery series?

8) How does Goff interweave ecological issues and concerns with her story? Were you aware of sun-grown vs. shade-grown coffee before reading *Death of a Songbird*?

9) Did *Death of a Songbird* raise your consciousness about ecological issues? Are you motivated to do anything about the demise of the songbird? Does the story make you want to know more about birds?

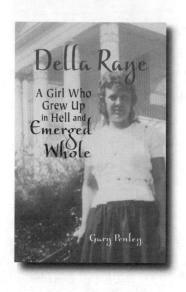

DELLA RAYE
A Girl Who Grew Up in Hell and Emerged Whole

Author: Gary Penley

Publisher: Pelican Publishing

Website: www.pelicanpub.com

Available in:
Hardcover, 240 pages. $22.00
(ISBN 1-56554-944-9)

Genre: Biography/
Coming of Age/Personal Triumph

Summary

For twenty years, Della Raye Rogers lived at the Partlow State Asylum for Mental Deficients in Tuscaloosa, Alabama. Left there by her uncle in 1929 at the age of four, along with her mother, aunt, and brother, she would know her mother only as another threat the attendants of the institution employed against her. She was subjected to beatings, made to work like a slave, and was given little formal education. Della Raye not only continued to hope and to fight, for her trials were not ended with her release, but she learned to forgive those who sought, by intent or by inaction, to destroy her.

Author Biography

Gary Penley had the idea to write Della Raye's story shortly after finishing his first novel, ***Rivers of Wind***. He met Della Raye's son Donny Hughes, who told him about his mother. They both knew that writing about her had to be his next project. Over the next year, he and Della met frequently as she told her entire story for the first time. Penley is a petroleum geologist. He lives in Sugar Land, Texas with his wife, Karen.

Topics to Consider

1) What personal convictions or characteristics enabled Della Raye to endure and overcome the twenty-year ordeal of confinement, abuse, and emotional neglect?

2) Could the same thing ever happen again? If you were in a similar situation, what would you do to insure your survival? Which of your own personality traits do you think would help you survive confinement?

3) What allowed such a thing to happen to a four-year-old girl who possessed a greater-than-average intelligence? How could she be committed to a mental institution, classified as an imbecile, and confined for twenty years?

4) Della Raye was not the only sane person locked in a mental institution during that time period; many were. What set her apart from others in the same situation?

5) When you think of situations in your life over which you have not had as much control as you would have liked, what did you draw on for strength?

6) The mental health care system has seen many changes since Della Raye was confined at Partlow. What aspects of mental health care do you feel have remained the same? What has changed? How have those changes affected society at large, or reflected changes in society?

7) The Great Depression was a tremendous influence on the course of Della Raye's life. What other historical events contributed to the conditions that gave rise to her confinement and its long duration? How did what was happening in the country after her release affect her adjustment to freedom?

8) Does Della Raye's ability to forgive inspire you to forgive? Do you feel her forgiveness was naïve, inspired, or necessary?

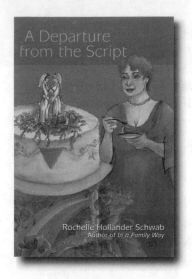

A DEPARTURE FROM THE SCRIPT

Author: Rochelle Hollander Schwab

Publisher: Orlando Place Press, 2002

Website: www.rochelleschwab.com

Available in:
Paperback, 328 pages. $14.95
(ISBN 0-9643650-1-4)

Genre: Fiction/
Family/Social Issues

Summary

Sheila Katz has it all: a successful amateur theater debut, a husband who looks like Robert Redford, and two wonderful grown children. True, her son became Catholic when he married—not a Jewish mother's dream. But Sheila is sure that any day now her daughter will announce her engagement to a wonderful Jewish boy. When the announcement comes though, there's one small change to Sheila's script: Jenny's intended is a wonderful Jewish girl. With assistance from a support group, Sheila rises to the occasion and helps Jenny plan a blowout lesbian wedding. Even as she calls caterers, Sheila is keeping the affair secret from her disapproving spouse. But another secret disturbs her far more: She has become infatuated with a striking lesbian artist. Now Sheila is dreaming of an affair of her own, one that could alter her life forever.

Recommended by: Stephen McCauley

"… A funny, lively writer who has something of importance to say about homophobia, acceptance, and family love … Will provide fodder for lively discussion about the many issues touched upon. Of equal importance, the novel's cast of sympathetic characters will stay with readers after they've finished the book."

Author Biography

Rochelle Schwab lives with her husband near Washington, DC, and is active in Parents, Families and Friends of Lesbians and Gays. That, and her relationship with her two daughters, spurred her to a fictional exploration of family issues. She's author of three previous novels; the last, ***In a Family Way***, was included in *Reading Group Choices 1997*.

Topics to Consider

1) At PFLAG support groups, like the one Sheila attends, parents of gays and lesbians often say that when their children come out of the closet, they go in. Why?

2) Do you have gay or lesbian family members or friends? How would you describe your family's reaction? How might you react if one of your children, or a close friend or family member, "came out" to you as lesbian or gay?

3) What are your feelings about Jenny and Tamara's ceremony? Should lesbians and gays be allowed to marry legally? Why or why not? If you were in a committed relationship with someone of your own sex, would you wish to be married?

4) When Dan tells Sheila that she is his best friend, her unspoken response is that friends are the women she talks to about her husband. Can a husband and wife be friends? What is a friend?

5) Are Sheila and Dan equal partners in their marriage? Why or why not?

6) Sheila manipulates Dan and hides her support for their daughter's ceremony from him. Under what circumstances, if any, are such deceptions justified in a relationship?

7) Both Jenny and Jeffrey deviated from the "script" that their parents had in mind for them: marriage to a Jewish partner of the opposite sex. Which disturbed Dan and Sheila more? Why?

8) Sheila experiences guilt after her brief "affair" with Naomi. Would she have felt more or less guilty if she had had an affair with someone of the opposite sex? How might Dan have felt if he had known about it? Do you see a difference in an affair with a person of the same sex compared to one of the opposite sex?

DIAMOND DOGS

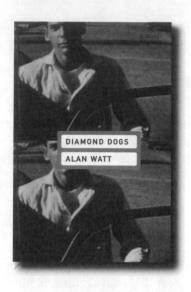

Author: Alan Watt

Publisher: Little, Brown & Co., 2001

Website: www.twbookmark.com

Available in:
Hardcover, 256 pages. $23.95
(ISBN 0-316-92581-0)

Genre: Fiction/
Relationships/Intrigue

Summary

Neil Garvin is a 17-year-old living in a small town outside of Las Vegas; abandoned by his mother when he was three, he blames his abusive father — who is the local sheriff — for driving her away. The quarterback of the high school football team, Neil is good-looking, popular, and as cruel to his peers as his father is to him. He plans to get out of town on his "million dollar arm," until the night when he accidentally commits a terrible crime, which his father, unasked, covers up for him. As the FBI arrives and begins to circle, Neil and his father become locked in a confrontation that will break them apart — and set them free.

Recommended by: *Kirkus Reviews*

"A powerful debut...Exquisite psychological fiction, resonating with suspense, wit, and perception."

Author Biography

Alan Watt was born in Scotland, raised in Canada, and moved to Los Angeles to pursue a career in stand up comedy. A movie that he wrote and directed is currently in production. ***Diamond Dogs*** is his first novel.

Topics to Consider

1) In the first chapter of the book, we see the main character behaving in ways that are not necessarily likeable. How do we become sympathetic to Neil?

2) Neil rebels against his father by rejecting the things that his father values such as his own name, and by embracing the things that his father hates. Why is football the exception?

3) How does the development of a group identity protect Neil? Do you think that this applies to young people in general?

4) Describe the conflicted relationships that develop between Burden, Neil, and Sheriff Garvin.

5) After Ian's death, Neil allows himself to become inappropriately intimate with the entire Curtis family. What is his motive for doing this?

6) How did his mother's leaving affect Neil's relationship with his father? How does it shape them individually?

7) Neil tends to see what he wants to see in regard to his mother. How does his discovery of the truth affect his perception of her?

8) Describe Neil's relationships with women. What purpose does Mary serve for him? For what purpose does he serve her? How do Lenore's actions contribute to Neil's feelings of guilt?

9) At the end of the book, does Neil understand his father better? Do you think either of them is redeemed? Do they deserve their punishments?

10) What kind of statement is **_Diamond Dogs_** making about American youth today?

Additional topics for discussion can be found at
www.twbookmark.com

EAST TO THE DAWN
The Life of Amelia Earhart

Author: Susan Butler

Publisher: Da Capo Press, 1999

Website: www.easttothedawn.com

Available in:
Paperback, 489 pages, $17.95
(ISBN 0-306-80887-0)

Genre: Biography/
History/Personal Challenges

Summary

With her all-American good looks, natural charm, and self-confidence, Amelia Earhart (1897-1937) captured the hearts of the entire nation after becoming the first woman to fly across the Atlantic Ocean in 1928. Yet, over half a century after her mysterious disappearance, many questions remained unanswered. Based on ten years of research through archives, letters, journals, and diaries, and on interviews with friends and relatives, this book includes intricate details about Earhart's career and her fateful last flight, with excerpts from letters written during the journey by her navigator Fred Noonan. The author also traces Earhart's personal life: her early years with her grandparents; her experiences as a nurse, pre-med student, business investor, and social worker; her famous marriage to publisher George Putnam; and her secret affair with Gene Vidal, head of the Bureau of Air Commerce. This biography presents a revealing picture of Earhart in all her complexity, and is sure to be the last word on her incredible life.

Recommended by: *Washington Post Book World*

"The single best book that we now have on Earhart's life."

Author Biography

Susan Butler—whose mother was a member of Amelia Earhart's flying organization, the Ninety-Nines—is a journalist whose work has appeared in *The New York Times* and other publications.

Topics to Consider

1) Did Amelia always want a career, even as a child? Do you think that is one of the secrets of her success?

2) Why is she such an icon? Do you think the fact that she was so photogenic has anything to do with it? Discuss the impact of her sudden death on the world. Does a violent death, accidental or not, add to a person's fame?

3) What was her most outstanding trait?

4) In her early twenties Earhart suggested that her parents invest in a gypsum mine, and she herself invested in a truck to deliver paving and building materials in Los Angeles. She later was involved in a variety of business ventures. How did she finally become a successful businesswoman?

5) Can you draw a meaningful parallel between Earhart's pursuit of economic goals and her pursuit of flying records?

6) Do you think she was lucky to have set so many flying records? Or was she a better pilot than the other women?

7) Discuss her last flight. Do you think Earhart and Noonan were foolhardy or careless? Does Butler's research convince you that the Electra went down into the sea?

8) What do you think Amelia would have done with the rest of her life, if she had lived?

9) If her plane is ever found, will that make her more famous, or less?

FLUX
Women on Sex, Work, Love, Kids, and Life in a Half-Changed World

Author: Peggy Orenstein

Publisher: Anchor Books, 2001

Website: www.vintagebooks.com/read

Available in:
Paperback, 352 pages. $14.00
(ISBN 0-385-49887-X)

Genre: Nonfiction/
Women's Studies/Personal Discovery

Summary

Peggy Orenstein's bestselling *Schoolgirls* is the classic study of teen-age girls and self-esteem. Now Orenstein uses the same interviewing and reporting skills to examine the lives of women in their 20s, 30s and 40s. The advances of the women's movement allow women to grow up with a sense of expanded possibilities. Yet traditional expectations have hardly changed. To discover how they are navigating this double burden personally and professionally, Orenstein interviewed hundreds of women and has blended their voices into a compelling narrative that gets deep inside their lives and choices. With unusual sensitivity, Orenstein offers insight and inspiration for every woman who is making important decisions of her own.

Recommended by: Anne Lamott, author of *Traveling Mercies*

"I loved it...It's brilliant, fascinating, touching, wonderfully composed."

Author Biography

Peggy Orenstein is the author of *Schoolgirls: Young Women, Self-Esteem, and the Confidence Gap*, which was a *New York Times* Notable Book. An award-winning writer and speaker on issues affecting girls and women, she is a regular contributor to *The New York Times Magazine*, and her work has also appeared in many other newspapers and magazines. She has also served as an editor at several notable magazines. Orenstein lives in Berkeley, California, with her husband, filmmaker Steven Okazaki.

Topics to Consider

1) Does contemporary society offer women more choices than those available to previous generations? Were our mothers and grandmothers more content than we are today?

2) Six female medical students discuss a seminar they'd just attended on balancing work and family. None of their male classmates came, nor did the women expect them to. What are the implications of the men's absence on the women's future careers and personal lives? What can women reasonably expect or demand from men?

3) Many of the working women in this book, whether they view themselves as being on the "fast track" or the "mommy track," reportedly feel that it is the women at work who judge them most harshly. Is this true in your experience? If so, why do you think this happens?

4) What role does money play in marriage? Is it the true source of power? Has your marriage ever undergone changes in the balance of power because of a dramatic change in the earning status of you or your spouse?

5) Orenstein notes that women, whatever their arrangements, feel like lesser mothers than those of the previous generation, while men, even with minimal participation at home, feel like better fathers. Do you think this is true? If so, why? What might change this?

6) Orenstein comments that women's endless attempts to be perfect mothers remind her of teenage girls, who, no matter what their weight, see themselves as fat. What does a mother have to do to feel "good enough"? What role does mother management play in what women consider good motherhood?

7) In what ways were the African American women's experiences different from the white women's in the book? Is there common ground between the experiences of these two different groups?

8) What can women do, personally and on a societal level, to get men to address the work-life dilemma, to struggle to maintain balance just as women do?

9) Have any of your opinions about marriage, kids, and work changed as a result of reading *Flux*? Has this book encouraged you to reevaluate your previous choices in any way?

FOUR LETTERS OF LOVE

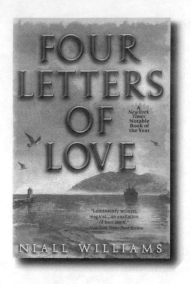

Author: Niall Williams

Publisher: Warner, 1998

Website: www.twbookmark.com

Available in:
Paperback, 275 pages, $13.99
(ISBN: 0-446-67493-1)

Genre: Fiction/
Relationships

Summary

Niall Williams has crafted a stunning novel of love and loss, madness and miracles, magic and reality. It is the story of Nicholas and Isabel, whose hearts were drawn by the winds of destiny. There was, after all, no reason for them to have met. He came from Dublin; she from a wild isle off the West Irish coast. Both, however, knew how lives could be shattered by the dawn of one day. In search of his artist father's lost masterwork, Nicholas would come to Isabel's door, and would find that passion had unexpectedly ignited his life...and hers. Blessed by fate, Nicholas and Isabel would learn that nothing in the world is random, that every step is measured, that every moment counts...and that time and envy are forces to be reckoned with.

Recommended by: *The New York Times Book Review*

*"A delicate and graceful love story that is also an exaltation of love itself ...
A luminously written, magical work of fiction."*

Author Biography

Niall Williams was born in Dublin in 1958. He is a playwright and the author of four books written with his wife, the artist Christine Breen, about their life in County Clare with their two children.

READING GROUP CHOICES

Topics to Consider

1) Several love stories unfold in the course of the novel. Compare Nicholas and Isabel's story with the courtships of Muiris and Margaret, William and Bette, and Isabel and Peader. Do you think this kind of fated love occurs in real life?

2) What purpose do the love letters from Nicholas to Isabel serve? Compare those letters with the love letters between other characters. Have you written or received love letters? How did they affect the relationship?

3) How do Nicholas's and Isabel's relationships with their parents affect their relationship? How do the parents' relationships affect their relationships with their children and their reactions to their children's love relationships? Is one kind of love — romantic or familial — more powerful than the other?

4) What is the role of God and religion in the characters' lives? Are the characters in control of their own destinies, or are they subject to larger forces?

5) The final line of the book states that "the plots of God and Love came together and were the same thing." Has the author's view of the influence of God changed through the course of the novel? Have the characters'? Has yours?

6) The book opens with William leaving his family, following, he believes, a command from God. But the pain this brings to his wife and son is immeasurable. How is it possible to balance responsibilities of family and home with your own, more personal, desire for fulfillment? Are you forced to give that up when you marry? When you become a parent?

7) All the love relationships (parent and child, brother and sister, husband and wife) in this book bring an incredible amount of pain into the characters' lives. Do you think this pain is necessary in order for them to experience joy?

8) In this book the creation of art is a powerful motivator — and a force of destruction. Do creation and destruction necessarily go hand in hand? Does the creation of art require suffering and sacrifice?

For additional topics, see www.twbookmark.com

Author: Anika Nailah

Publisher: Doubleday, 2002

Website: www.doubleday.com

Available in:
Hardcover, 224 pages. $21.95
(ISBN 0-385-50293-1)

Genre: Fiction/
Personal Challenges/Social Issues

Summary

Anika Nailah illuminates the emotional, spiritual, and social realities that shape—and sometimes destroy—the lives and dreams of ordinary African Americans. The stories in *Free* offer an original perspective on how cultural experiences and social assumptions impact our lives. "Trudy" depicts a battle of wills between a black salesclerk and a white customer, shining a harsh light on the bigotry of the 1950s. "All These Years" is a vignette about a couple married for fifty-four years who reminisce about the attraction they felt at their very first meeting. In "Inside Out," a man who has adopted all the trappings of the white world finds himself still ostracized in his office and gently mocked at home by a wife who embraces her blackness with pride. Nailah exposes the injustices and struggles African Americans confront, the skills they develop in order to survive, and the psychological and spiritual costs of survival.

Recommended by: David Anthony Durham, author of *Gabriel's Story*

"The stories in Free *are plainspoken, understated and deceptively complex. Anika Nailah makes everyday interactions between black and white, young and old, into capsules of insight."*

Author Biography

Anika Nailah, a freelance writer and literacy consultant, is the director of Books of Hope, a program that encourages young people to write and self-publish their own books. She lives in Massachusetts.

Topics to Consider

1) What theme or themes do you think tie these stories together?

2) Which story or stories had the greatest impact on you? Why?

3) In "Trudy," we are immediately caught up in a disagreement between a retail employee and a customer. Discuss how the story might change if told by a different character, for example, the white customer? Or, if it were told today and not 1954?

4) In "My Side of the Story," Eddie uses the word "ugly" several times to describe things around him. Why is everything ugly to Eddie? What is the symbolism in Eddie's allowing Malcolm's leash to fall into the lake?

5) Several characters in the book are children trying to cope with the mysteries of adult behavior, people who have allowed society to define who they are, and others who are trying to live with the difficult choices they have made. In particular, one thread seems to focus on women and issues of abandonment. What is the significance of the women in some of the stories leaving their marriages and families after so many years?

6) What does the author mean by the words, "Silence, a familiar guest, pulled up a chair" on p. 73 in "All These Years?"

7) Religion and vivid colors stand out when contrasted with the drab setting in "Sunday Visit." What do religion and colors represent?

8) How does the author convey the importance we place on beauty through "Deena?"

9) In the story "Free" what can you deduce about the woman Paula's mother was before she left her husband, and the person she appeared to be in the latter part of her life? Why was Paula the only one that could sense her mother? Who is free, Paula or her mother? Why?

A Reading Group Companion is available at:
www.randomhouse.com/resources/rgg.html

THE HEARTSONG OF CHARGING ELK

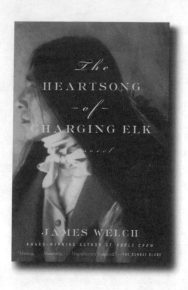

Author: James Welch

Publisher: Anchor Books, 2001

Website: www.vintagebooks.com/read

Available in:
Paperback, 448 pages. $14.00
(ISBN 0-385-49675-3)

Genre: Fiction/Literature/
Personal Challenges/Social Issues

Summary

Charging Elk, an Oglala Sioux, joins Buffalo Bill's Wild West Show and journeys from the Black Hills of South Dakota to the back streets of nineteenth-century Marseille. Left behind in a Marseille hospital after a serious injury while the show travels on, he is forced to remake his life alone in a strange land. He struggles to adapt as well as he can, while holding on to the memories and traditions of life on the Plains and eventually falling in love. But none of the worlds the Indian has known can prepare him for the betrayal that follows. This is a story of the American Indian that we have seldom seen: a stranger in a strange land, often an invisible man, loving, violent, trusting, wary, protective, and defenseless against a society that excludes him but judges him by its rules.

Recommended by: *The Sunday Globe*

"Moving ... Absorbing ... Magnificently imagined."

Author Biography

James Welch attended schools on the Blackfeet and Fort Belknap reservations in Montana, and studied writing at the University of Montana. One of his four previous novels, **Fools Crow,** won the *Los Angeles Times* Book Award and the Pacific Northwest Booksellers Award. Welch lives in Missoula, Montana, with his wife, Lois.

Topics to Consider

1) Can *The Heartsong of Charging Elk* be read as an allegory of the Sioux Native Americans' adjustment to life on the reservation? How does Charging Elk's situation in Marseille differ? If the novel is allegorical, what do each of the characters in the novel represent?

2) Is Charging Elk aware of the irony that while he performs in a stage show that glorifies the defeat of the white man, in reality the white man is slowly changing the Indian's way of life?

3) Why does Welch describe Charging Elk's memories of America instead of describing his emotions? Does this narrative device affect the reader's ability to sympathize with Charging Elk? Why might the author want to distance the reader from Charging Elk at certain pivotal moments in the story?

4) How does Charging Elk overcome the paradox of looking so different physically, and yet feeling "invisible"? Is this symbolic of a larger theme of racial inequality?

5) What is the significance of the refrain from Charging Elk's dream which echoes throughout the second half of the novel: "You are my only son" [p. 252]? What is the "heartsong" of Charging Elk, and does it change or evolve over the course of the novel?

6) What statements does the novel make about the dangers of assimilation? Is it necessary for an individual to lose something of his original culture in order to become assimilated into a new culture?

7) From Charging Elk's point of view, what is the difference between being inside the church, where it is "warm and holy," [p. 67] and being back at home celebrating religious rituals in Lakota? Is religion simply a matter of personal reality, as Charging Elk thinks when he realizes, "Wakan Tanka was not here in this land, had never been here! All those times he had prayed to the Great Mystery had been futile" [p. 427]?

HONKY

Honky

"A wonderful book about growing up . . . as a white kid in a largely poor black and Hispanic neighborhood. . . . A triumph."
—Jonathan Lethem, author of *Motherless Brooklyn*

Dalton Conley

Author: **Dalton Conley**

Publisher: Vintage Books, 2001

Website: www.vintagebooks.com/read

Available in:
Paperback, 224 pages. $12.00
(ISBN 0-375-72775-2)

Genre: Biography/
Personal Challenges/Social Issues

Summary

Dalton Conley's childhood has all of the classic elements of growing up in America. But the fact that he was one of the few white boys in a mostly black and Puerto Rican neighborhood on Manhattan's Lower East Side makes Dalton's childhood unique. At the age of three, he couldn't understand why the infant daughter of the black separatists next door couldn't be his sister, so he kidnapped her. By the time he was a teenager, he realized that not even a parent's devotion could protect his best friend from a stray bullet. Years after the privilege of being white and middle class allowed Conley to leave the projects, his illuminating memoir allows us to see how race and class impact us all. Perfectly pitched and daringly original, *Honky* is that rare book that entertains even as it informs.

Recommended by: Jonathan Lethem, author of *Motherless Brooklyn*

"A wonderful book about growing up...as a white kid in a largely poor black and hispanic neighborhood...A triumph."

Author Biography

Dalton Conley is Associate Professor of Sociology and Director of the Center for Advanced Social Science Research at New York University. Previously he taught in the departments of Sociology and African American Studies at Yale University. He is the author of *Being Black, Living in the Red: Race, Wealth, and Social Policy in America*.

Topics to Consider

1) How much do you think Conley's parents' decision to live in the projects was a matter of choice and how much was it out of their control?

2) Conley says that "race and class are nothing more than a set of stories we tell ourselves to get through the world, to organize our reality" [p. xiv]. Do you believe that race and class can be treated as subjective rather than fixed and objective categories?

3) What are the most significant insights that **Honky** offers? In what ways is Conley's firsthand experience more valuable than scientific data?

4) After Conley accidentally sets fire to his friend Raphael's apartment, he realizes, "Had the fire not been in Chelsea but down the street from our house in one of the row tenements that lined Avenue D—or had I been of a different skin tone—the whole matter might not have been settled so casually" [p. 181]. What other experiences make Conley aware of his privileged status as a white person? What effect do these revelations have on him?

5) What coping strategy does Conley employ after the shooting of his best friend, Jerome? What does he try to achieve through this behavior? What does it suggest about the effects of living in a violent environment on young children?

6) In what ways do the media and society construct the narratives of blacks and other minorities in America? What are those narratives? What purposes do they serve for the dominant ethnic group? What effects do they have on minorities?

7) What does Conley discover about race and class when he changes from P.S. 4 in the projects to P.S. 41 in the West Village? Do you find fault with his parents for lying about their address to the school board? Why or why not?

8) In what ways does **Honky** illustrate, rather than merely assert, the privileges that even poor whites like the Conleys can enjoy in the United States? Why is Conley, unlike most of his neighbors in the projects, able to get a first-rate education and a prestigious job?

A HUNDRED WAYS TO SUNDAY

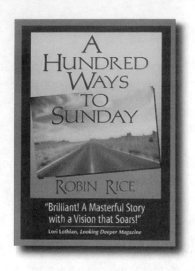

"Brilliant! A Masterful Story with a Vision that Soars!"
Lori Lothian, *Looking Deeper Magazine*

Author: Robin Rice

Publisher: Be Who You Are Press, 2001

Website: www.BeWhoYouAre.com

Available in:
Paperback, 238 pages, $13.95.
(ISBN 0-9710876-4-4)

Genre: Fiction/
Inspiration & Faith/Personal Discovery

Summary

Mary Margaret Hathaway has been told by shamans the world over that she is *The One.* If only they had been willing to tell her what *The One* is supposed to do. Following synchronicities like bread crumbs, she comes to her true beginning in Canyon de Chelly, Arizona. With the desert to test her, she meets teachers in the form of a 5-year-old boy, a 108-year-old man, and a host of others in between. A story of the arduous journey to becoming who we really are, *A Hundred Ways to Sunday* offers hope for everyone who believes there is something more to this world than what our five senses can reveal.

Recommended by: Denise Baddour, *ContentConnect*

"...a storytelling power reminiscent of a Paulo Coelho adventure. Rice weaves a visionary tale of the soul's quest for truth with characters so real they seem to escape into form and stay there."

Author Biography

Robin Rice is a multi-published author and contemporary shaman. Her passion is telling stories that reveal the nobility of the true heart, the pain of the human condition, and the miraculous power of the Divine to heal us all.

Topics to Consider

1) The author uses the title in a casual remark by Mary. What is the full meaning of the title?

2) Many "New Age" ideas are presented in the book, yet many messages from the book have a root in Christianity. How do these ideas blend? How do they clash?

3) Chief suggests that past lives are not real, because the past and future are not real. Yet he knows that Mary must journey to her past lives to heal herself. How can both be true?

4) Kenya suggests an ice cream metaphor to justify her position on fear. Is fear the true root of fidelity issues? Why would the author choose this particular topic to make her point about fear?

5) Why does Mary identify with Dark Crow's *Nothin'*? How can this world offer so much and yet leave people like Mary feeling as if they are drowning in *Nothin'*?

6) Author Jean Perkins said of the book "It offers hope that our struggles really do have a purpose." What is the purpose of Mary's struggles? Our own?

7) Robin Rice is quoted as saying "I wanted to write fiction that stands alone as quality fiction, whether you embrace Mary's version of spirituality or not." In what ways did she accomplish this task? In what ways did she fail?

8) In one of her journeys, Mary uses psychotropic drugs. Is the author condoning such use? Could drug abuse be related to our desire for out of body experiences? Where is the line to be drawn between using drugs for recreation, spiritual enlightenment, and out of a destructive habit?

9) Mothering issues are found throughout the book, from Mother Earth to Wyunetta Morningstar to Mary's giving up motherhood for Lent. What is the author trying to say?

10) If, as Chief suggests, we choose our parents, and even our life tragedies prior to them occurring, does that make life predestined? What does that say about our choices within this lifetime?

INFIDELITY

Author: Ann Pearlman

Publisher: Broadway Books, 2001

Website: www.broadwaybooks.com

Available in:
Paperback, 253 pages. $14.00
(ISBN 0-7679-0811-2)

Genre: Biography/
Relationships

Summary

It is estimated that an alarming four out of five married couples experience infidelity. Growing up with a mother and grandmother who painfully accepted the existence of their respective husbands' mistresses, Ann Pearlman set out to beat the odds. She embarked on a career as a therapist who helped hundreds of unhappily married patients build new lives. She also found a husband with whom she felt secure. But after thirty years of rewarding marriage and parenthood, she discovered that her husband was having an affair with one of his art students. *Infidelity* is the moving account of her shattered trust, and the women in her family who endured similar wounds in the radically different climate of America before 1960.

Recommended by: *Oakland Press*

"Ann Pearlman has handled infidelity with a sense of humor and a delicacy that could break the heart."

Author Biography

Ann Pearlman is a marriage and family therapist and the author of two previous books. She has appeared on numerous national television shows and contributed to *O, The Oprah Magazine*. She lives in Ann Arbor, Michigan.

Topics to Consider

1) The first chapter details an early moment of sibling rivalry and jealousy. What light does Pearlman's behavior as a three-year-old shed on the phenomenon of adultery? What lessons does the young Ann learn from her attempted fratricide?

2) In what ways does Jake's behavior destabilize the family home? What lessons does Ann learn about being a wife from her own mother?

3) Why do you think the women of Ann's family all wind up with unfaithful spouses with addictive personalities?

4) How do the households in Ann's extended family hide their secrets? At what point in her life does Ann begin to discover the deceit that lies beneath her parents' marriage?

5) Do the anonymous phone calls regarding Jake's affair with Donna change anything? Who do you think made those calls, and why? If you received a similar call, accusing your spouse of cheating on you, how would you respond?

6) To what use does Ann put her powers of persuasion and seduction? How is she similar to her father?

7) Why do you think so many people crave monogamy from their partners and themselves, yet there is so much infidelity in the world?

8) How do the different generations of women in Ann's family cope with their husbands' infidelities? Do their coping methods reflect generational differences?

9) How do you think the women in Ann's family could avoid blaming themselves for their husbands' infidelities? Is it possible for them to put a stop to their husbands' affairs?

10) How does Ann change herself to be Ty's mate? Do you think the breakup of their marriage could have been avoided?

11) How is Ann able to recover from Ty's infidelity? What are the steps she goes through in order to go on with her life?

Additional topics for discussion can be found at the back of the book.

THE JEW STORE

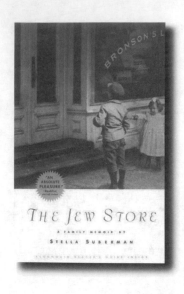

Author: Stella Suberman

Publisher: Algonquin Books, 2000

Website: www.Algonquin.com

Available in:
Paperback, 298 pages. $13.95
(ISBN 1-56512-330-1)

Genre: Biography/
Personal Challenges/Social Issues

Summary

The Bronsons were the first Jews ever to live in the small town of Concordia, Tennessee. That didn't stop Aaron Bronson, a Russian immigrant, from moving his family out of New York by horse and wagon in 1920 and journeying to this remote corner of the South to open a small dry goods store. Never mind that he was greeted with "Danged if I ever heard tell of a Jew storekeeper afore." Never mind that all the townspeople were suspicious of any strangers. Never mind that the Klan actively discouraged the presence of outsiders. Aaron Bronson bravely established a business, and proved in the process that his family could make a home, and a life, anywhere. This is a family story that speaks to the immigrant experience of millions of Americans.

Recommended by: *The New York Times Book Review*

"Like the store, which is practically a character in its own right, the people in **The Jew Store** *linger in the mind."*

Author Biography

Stella Suberman was born in a small Bible Belt town in Tennessee to which her family had come in 1920 to open a dry goods store. She has lived in North Carolina and Florida, serving as a staff book reviewer for the *Miami Herald*. **The Jew Store** was selected by the Women's National Book Association as one of five recommended books for 2000.

Topics to Consider

1) Aaron took his family to a place where he knew they would be outsiders, if not outcasts. Do you see that decision as a courageous one, or one that was inherently selfish and foolhardy?

2) What's your impression of Miss Brookie? With her education and worldliness, why did she continue to live in Concordia?

3) Miss Brookie and Aaron Bronson have very different explanations for why the Klan did not march on the Bronsons' store. Why do you think the KKK chose not to march?

4) What were Sadie's reasons for discouraging the marriage between Hannah and Manny? Do you think they were valid? To what extent would this kind of thinking prevail today?

5) Concordia was hit hard by the Great Depression. What lingering effects has the Depression had on you, your parents, or your grandparents?

6) What did you make of Aaron's ability to turn his Jewishness into an asset during the pledge night for the factory?

7) What do you think would have happened if Miriam had married T? How would Concordia have reacted? How would Reba and Aaron have taken it?

8) Reba and Aaron were in conflict over leaving Concordia. Who did you end up siding with, and why?

9) Did the account of how Aaron left Russia and came to America trigger any stories you may have heard from your own family?

10) How do you feel about Stella Suberman's use of racial slurs within the text? Why do you think she chose to use derogatory terms rather than more appropriate contemporary language?

Additional topics for discussion can be found at the back of the book.

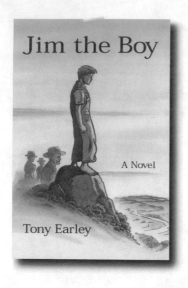

JIM THE BOY

Author: Tony Earley

Publisher: Back Bay Books, 2001

Website: www.twbookmark.com

Available in:
Paperback, 239 pages, $12.95
(ISBN 0-316-19895-1)

Genre: Fiction/
Coming of Age

Summary

Jim is a 10-year-old boy growing up in the Depression-era town of Aliceville, North Carolina, with his widowed mother and her three bachelor brothers. He plays baseball, attends a new school, and befriends a rival, all the while measuring himself against the high standards set by his mother and uncles and the long shadows cast by his dead father. As he takes the first tentative steps toward the bittersweet boundary marking the end of his childhood, Jim becomes increasingly aware of the complex adult world that shelters him and of his desire to see what the rest of the world holds.

Recommended by: Ellen Currie, *The New York Times Book Review*

"Tony Earley has a wonderful gift for deep observation, exact and wise and often funny."

Author Biography

Selected by Granta as one of today's best young novelists and featured in *The New Yorker's* best young fiction issue, **Tony Earley** is one of today's most important writers. He was raised in Rutherfordton, NC, and attended the University of Alabama at Tuscaloosa, where he earned his M.F.A. in creative writing and won several fiction prizes. He has taught writing at Carnegie Mellon, The University of the South, and is currently an Assistant Professor of English at Vanderbilt University.

Topics to Consider

1) How do Jim's uncles each play the role of father-figure? Do they make up for his father's absence? Should Jim's mother have remarried when she had the chance in order to give Jim a "real" father?

2) Both the setting and Jim's life have a simple quality, yet through each flows a more complicated undercurrent. How do the setting and era reflect Jim's character?

3) Why does Uncle Zeno take Jim on the trip out of town? What do the incident with the horses and his first view of the ocean teach him?

4) Jim's mother turned down the marriage proposal because she believed she had already met and married her one eternal love. Do you believe, as she does, in the idea of eternal love?

5) Why did Jim feel such a strong sense of rivalry toward Penn? What in their pasts and their families' pasts connected them?

6) Jim has moments of selfishness. How does he begin to take responsibility for his actions as he grows older?

7) In just one year, both Jim and the United States experienced tremendous change. How does Earley incorporate the evolving society into Jim's story? Think about education, the economy, electricity, transportation, race relations, and polio. What will Jim experience that his uncles and mother never did? How will his adult world differ from theirs?

8) What role does Abraham play? What lessons does he teach Jim, both in the field and in the alley?

9) What is the significance of the final scene with Jim's grandfather and his two cousins? What realizations does Jim have during this scene?

10) Think about the stories that are told about Jim's father. What is Jim's vision of the kind of man his father was?

For additional topics, see www.twbookmark.com

LEAVING KATYA

Author: Paul Greenberg

Publisher: G.P. Putnam's Sons, 2002

Website: www.leavingkatya.com

Available in:
Hardcover, 320 pages. $24.95
(ISBN 0-399-14835-3)

Genre: Fiction/
Personal Challenges/Relationships

Summary

A one-night stand with an enigmatic Russian woman might seem like the stuff of fantasy, but for Daniel it is just the beginning of a nightmarish descent into a shattering crisis of character. *Leaving Katya*, Paul Greenberg's bittersweet tale of love and loss, traces the arc of a relationship struggling to survive in the no man's land between two intensely different cultures. From the beginning of their affair, Daniel tries to deduce whether Katya is the love of his life or just another part of what his psychiatrist father calls "The Russia Phase." Before he can sift through it all, however, events overtake him. The Soviet Union falls, Katya flees Leningrad, and soon she is smack dab in the middle of Daniel's New York slacker existence. In short, if *Catcher in the Rye*'s Holden Caulfield were to marry Anna Karenina, things might have gone something like this.

Recommended by: Darcy Frey, *New York Times Magazine*

"a heartbreakingly good book...Greenberg writes as grippingly about the world of geopolitics as he does about the inner turmoil of his characters."

Author Biography

Paul Greenberg worked in the Ex-USSR and Eastern Europe throughout the 1990s. Fluent in Russian, Greenberg taught journalism in Siberia, ran television management seminars in Tajikistan, and produced cross-cultural news magazines in Bosnia and Kosovo. A full-time novelist and screenwriter since 1998, Greenberg has written for television's *Invisible Man* and is currently at work on his next novel, ***The Retreat***.

Topics to Consider

1) Are Katya's and Daniel's misunderstandings Russian-American misunderstandings or are they classic conflicts that always occur between men and women?

2) Why do men like Daniel fall for mysterious, enigmatic women like Katya?

3) Dreams appear throughout *Leaving Katya* both as harbingers of things to come and as a kind of second channel of communication for Daniel and Katya. Where is the real communication happening between the couple — in waking life or in dreams?

4) How does Daniel's and Katya's sexual intimacy reflect the changes in their relationship?

5) Being the son of a psychiatrist, Daniel has grown up with a Freudian take on love and family. Why then is Katya's dismissal of Freud, psychiatry and psychotherapy so appealing to him? Is Russian love a purer form of love?

6) Does Daniel really have a weak character? Does Katya have a strong character? How does the concept of character differ in Russia and America?

7) Why does Katya seek out the Sri Vishnu Brahmaputra?

8) Which classic classic works of Russian literature are alluded to in *Leaving Katya*?

9) Is Daniel in the end a sympathetic character? Does Katya really love him?

10) How does Daniel's and Katya's relationship mirror the relationship between the United States and Russia in the post-Cold War era?

Simple Reminders for Finding Balance in a *24-7* World

life is not
work
work is not
LIFE

ROBERT K. JOHNSTON
& J. WALKER SMITH

LIFE IS NOT WORK, WORK IS NOT LIFE

**Authors: Robert K. Johnston, Ph.D. &
J. Walker Smith, Ph.D.**

Publisher: Wildcat Canyon Press, 2001

Website: www.wildcatcanyon.com

Available in:
Paperback, 256 pages. $13.95
(ISBN 1-885171-54-4)

Genre: Nonfiction/
Personal Discovery/Work Life

Summary

In no small way, the 20th Century was defined by work: Industrialization. Glass ceilings. Downsizing. In the new century, we would do well to remember that in order to support our work ethic, we need to refresh ourselves. And even more important, we need to find a balance between work and the rest of life. This book of mini-essays quiets the frenzy that seems to have all of us working longer and enjoying life less. To compelling quotes and statistics, the authors have added wisdom that will nourish, challenge, and surprise you. This is the perfect book for those who work hard, yet are looking to find that needed balance in their life.

Recommended by: Beth Sawi, CAO of Charles Schwab & Co.

"...Thought-provoking yet easy to absorb. The perfect antidote to today's overbooked world."

Author Biographies

Robert K. Johnston, Ph.D., currently Professor of Theology and Culture at Fuller Theological Seminary in Pasadena, California, is the author or co-author of nine books as well as more than 80 articles and chapters on topics such as theology and literature, theology and film and the Old Testament.

J. Walker Smith, Ph.D., is president of Yankelovich Partners, a branding and marketing consultancy specializing in lifestyle trends and customer targeting solutions. He lives in Atlanta, GA.

Topics to Consider

1) Why has the workweek increased to 47 hours per week over the last two decades, following a century-long decline?

2) Do you feel that your life is out of balance in favor of work? If so, has it gotten more or less balanced as you have gotten older?

3) Rob Johnston describes limits that he puts on his work life: not answering email every day, refusing to own a cell phone, not working on vacation. What steps, if any, do you take to limit work in your life? Do you get resistance to these steps from others?

4) Do you think that Americans work harder than people in other cultures? Why or why not?

5) Do you feel it's possible to limit work and also be professionally successful?

6) Do you have a role model in your life for work-life balance? Who is this person?

7) In one study, 36 percent of people polled wanted more money, while 64 percent wanted more time. Given the choice, which would you prefer?

8) Is multi-tasking effective?

9) Do you think there is a link between women's increased presence in the workplace and the longer workweek?

10) Generally speaking, do you sleep when you are tired, eat when you are hungry, or listen to other body signals?

11) If you would term yourself a "workaholic" (or others in your life would classify you as one), what is the motivator for such devotion to work?

12) According to a Gallup poll, 78 percent of Americans feel the need to experience spiritual growth; yet there is an increase in "cheating" tolls, restaurants and other facilities, as well as an increase in road and air rage incidents. How can this contradiction be explained?

LOOK AT ME

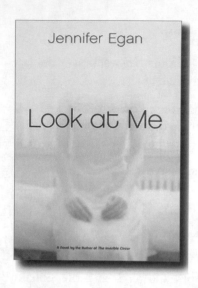

Author: Jennifer Egan

Publisher: Nan A. Talese/
Doubleday, 2001

Website: www.nanatalese.com

Available in:
Hardcover, 432 pages, $24.95
(ISBN: 0-385-50276-1)

Genre: Fiction/
Personal Challenges

Summary

Fashion model Charlotte Swenson returns to Manhattan, having just recovered from a catastrophic car accident in her hometown of Rockford, Illinois. Her career already in a downward spiral, the resultant facial surgery leaves her unrecognizable to friends and acquaintances alike. Finding it impossible to resume her former life, she floats invisibly through an ephemeral world of fashion nightclubs and Internet projects. While recovering in Rockford, she had met another Charlotte, the plain-looking teenage daughter of her former best friend, and a cast of other seemingly disparate characters. At the close of the novel, we are asked to examine the furious pace of modern life and the price it requires we pay.

Recommended by: *The New Yorker*

"A comic, richly imagined, and stunningly written exploration of the American obsession with self-invention."

Author Biography

Jennifer Egan is the author of ***The Invisible Circus***, and the short story collection ***Emerald City***. Her nonfiction appears frequently in *The New York Times Magazine*. She lives with her husband and son in New York City.

Topics to Consider

1) How is Charlotte's chosen path a reaction to her place of birth? What does her return to Rockford at the end of the book signify?

2) Talk about Charlotte's notion of the "shadow self." What do you imagine her shadow self looking like? How does it change after her accident?

3) Discuss the transformations that many of the characters in the story have undergone. In what specific ways do people change, and what do these changes mean?

4) Why do you think Charlotte would not allow any of her friends to see her while she was recuperating from surgery? Would you have felt any different?

5) Recognitions and misunderstandings play a crucial role in the plot. Identify some of these misunderstandings, and talk about their significance to the novel as a whole.

6) Discuss Charlotte's relationship with Irene Maitlock; what is it about Irene that draws Charlotte to her? How does their relationship change over the course of the book?

7) Discuss Egan's characters' relationships to memory. What connection does the novel suggest between personal memory and cultural memory? How do you suppose young Charlotte might feel about her memories, twenty years down the road?

8) The novel seems intentionally to leave us without a clear sense of what kinds of lives the characters will go on to lead. Why do you think Egan has chosen to end her book so ambiguously? What sort of lives do you think the characters will go on to live?

9) With its depiction of behind-the-scenes events in the making of public images, will this book have any impact on the way you look at famous people?

10) Do you consider *Look at Me* a futuristic novel? Or do you read it as a fairly accurate look at our present, evolving world?

Additional topics for discussion can be found at:
www.randomhouse.com/resources/rgg.html

LYING AWAKE

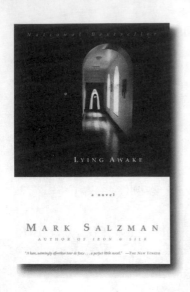

Author: **Mark Salzman**

Publisher: Vintage Books, 2001

Website: www.vintagebooks.com/read

Available in:
Paperback, 192 pages. $12.00
(ISBN 0-375-70606-2)

Genre: Fiction/Inspiration &
Faith/Personal Challenges

Summary

Sister John's cloistered life of peace and prayer has been electrified by ever more frequent visions of God's radiance, leading her toward a deep religious ecstasy. Her life and writings have become examples of devotion. Yet her visions are accompanied by shattering headaches that compel Sister John to seek medical help. When her doctor tells her an illness may be responsible for her gift, Sister John faces a wrenching choice: to risk her intimate glimpses of the divine in favor of a cure, or to continue her visions with the knowledge that they might be false—and might even cost her her life.

Recommended by: *The New Yorker*

"A lean, seemingly effortless tour de force … a perfect little novel."

Author Biography

Mark Salzman is the author of *Iron & Silk*, an account of his two years in China; the novels *The Laughing Sutra* and *The Soloist*, which was a finalist for the *Los Angeles Times* Book Prize for fiction; and *Lost in Place*, a memoir. He lives in Los Angeles with his wife, filmmaker Jessica Yu.

Topics to Consider

1) How appropriate is the choice of locale of the monastery of Sisters of the Carmel of Saint Joseph in the very heart of Los Angeles rather than in a more pastoral setting?

2) The nuns follow a way of life established for centuries. In what ways, if any, are they allowed to express their individuality?

3) The story of Sister John's past unfolds gradually throughout the novel. In what ways did her family situation and her attachment to her teacher, Sister Priscilla, influence her decision to become a nun? Is she drawn to the religious life for spiritual reasons alone, or do other aspects of her life play an equally important part?

4) "For seven years she watched as the cloister got smaller and the silence got bigger ... and the farther she traveled inward without finding Him, the more aware she became of His absence" [p. 97-98]. How does Sister John's period of spiritual aridity affect the decision she must later make about her medical condition?

5) Sister John wonders whether Dostoevsky would have been treated for his epilepsy if he had had the option. In view of his description of his rapture [p. 120], how would you answer this question? Can artistic inspiration be related to mental imbalances, either physical or psychological? For example, how did the mental instability of artists and writers such as Vincent Van Gogh, Robert Lowell, and Sylvia Plath influence their work?

6) Why does the priest say, "We're all better off having doubts about the state of our souls than presuming ourselves to be holy" [p. 125]? How does this compare to the teachings of most religion and most people's beliefs? To what extent do our behavior and the decisions we make entail making "presumptions" about ourselves and our place in the world?

7) "I made a commitment to live by faith, not by reason," writes Sister John [p. 119]. In making her decision about surgery, does she rely entirely on faith, or does reason play a role as well?

8) What details of daily life in the monastery help to establish the themes Salzman is exploring?

MAN AND BOY

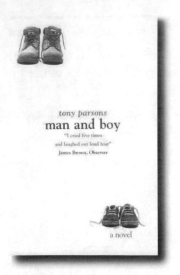

Author: Tony Parsons

Publisher: Scribner, 2002 (May)

Website: www.SimonSays.com

Available in:
Paperback, 368 pages. $12.00
(ISBN 0-7432-2508-2)

Genre: Fiction/
Family/Personal Triumph

Summary

Harry Silver has a successful job in TV, a gorgeous wife, a lively child. But as he approaches his 30th birthday, things start to get out of control. He's obsessed with getting older, and in a foolish moment of flirtation with an attractive co-worker, he sacrifices his perfect life. His wife leaves him, he loses his job to the colleague he slept with, and he finds himself facing the mind-boggling challenge of being a single, unemployed parent to his son. *Man and Boy* is the story of how his unexpected role helps Harry come to terms with his life, better appreciate his own father, a decorated WWII veteran, and achieve a degree of self-respect. It is an unforgettable story of love, infidelity, family, death, and new beginnings.

Recommended by: *USA Today*

*"Set your other books aside for a day or two and read straight through **Man and Boy**."*

Author Biography

Tony Parsons, one of the most well-known journalists in England, is a columnist for the *Mirror* and also writes for *The Guardian, The Spectator,* and *The Sunday Times.* He lives in London, England.

Topics to Consider

1) Did **Man and Boy** change any of your feelings about the kind of love a father feels for his child? How is the love a father has for his son or daughter different from the love a mother feels?

2) How well did the story succeed in showing how the love of a family passes down from generation to generation?

3) Does Harry want to be an "old-school dad" like his father, or a new kind of father, husband and man?

4) Is the story gender specific? Would it work equally well if it were about a woman being left to bring up her daughter alone while attempting to resolve her sometimes difficult relationship with her mother?

5) How does Harry's parenting ability change during the course of the story? What is a good parent in the context of **Man and Boy**?

6) Harry is an incurable romantic. Is it dangerous for a man to be that addicted to romance? Why does it lead him into trouble and grief? Are men really bigger romantics than women?

7) How does Harry's relationship with his father change when he learns that his dad is terminally ill? How does Harry's father deal with his illness?

8) Does the book have a happy ending? Do you feel that the relationship between Cyd and Harry will last? What has Harry's divorce taught him?

9) Why does Harry's wife leave him—because of his sexual betrayal, or because he has broken some greater trust? If Gina had not discovered his infidelity, would they have still had a "good" marriage? What is a "good" marriage?

10) What does this book tell us about single parents? Are single fathers different from single mothers?

11) Does **Man and Boy** have any heroes? Is Harry a heroic figure? Is Harry's father? Is Gina?

12) Is **Man and Boy** a book about the rights of children?

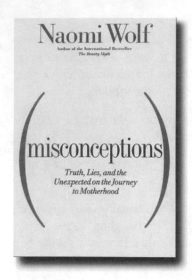

MISCONCEPTIONS

Author: Naomi Wolf

Publisher: Doubleday, 2001

Website: www.doubleday.com

Available in:
Hardcover, 336 pages. $24.95
(ISBN 0-385-49302-9)

Genre: Nonfiction/
Social Issues/Women's Studies

Summary

Examining everything from the maternity smock to the episiotomy, from the infertility clinic to the play group, from midwife to medical insurance, *Misconceptions* reveals how the things we've been taught to expect of pregnancy, childbirth, and even mother love might prove not just off base but downright dangerous. In her signature style, Naomi Wolf infuses her questions and their well-researched and thought-provoking answers with a voice that is by turns political and personal. Writer, activist, and mother, Wolf reveals the sometimes precarious transitions any woman is asked to make as she moves from role to role, finding, along the way, the points where these disparate selves might meet and reconcile.

Recommended by: Gloria Steinem

" Combines intimate experience and exposé reporting ... Everyone who is giving birth or getting health care should read this book."

Author Biography

Naomi Wolf is the author of the best-selling *The Beauty Myth*, which helped to launch a new wave of feminism in the early 1990s and was named one of the most significant books of the twentieth century by the *New York Times*. More recently she has authored *Fire with Fire* and *Promiscuities*. She lives in New York City with her family.

Topics to Consider

1) Discuss how a diagnosis of postpartum depression, or the condition itself, affected you or people you know. Why do you suppose the incidence is so high in this country, and so much lower in others?

2) Wolf claims that motherhood has been sentimentalized in our culture. Explore the ways in which a charming, rosy picture of pregnancy and parenthood might trivialize this challenging experience. End your discussion with a quick look at maternity clothes.

3) What is it that most assures that one person's life might be free of fatalism while another person's life seems to depend on it?

4) Discuss the "will and longing" that Wolf feels played a role in her conception while on birth control. Wolf holds the light of folklore to the light of the scientific, and vice versa. Where do you stand?

5) Discuss the several shifts in her political thinking that accompanied Wolf's pregnancy, and describe similar shifts that may have accompanied yours if you have ever been pregnant. Do you consider such shifts to constitute a loss of self? Why? Why not?

6) Even prior to labor, some women actively elect to have C-sections. For what reasons do you imagine a woman might make such a decision?

7) In addition to the medical establishment, the insurance industry, and the legal industry, what are some of the other institutions that you feel exercise significant influence, undue or otherwise, on women in labor?

8) How do you suppose your grandmother would react to this book?

9) How might things be different if men were the ones to bear children?

A Reading Group Companion is available at:
www.randomhouse.com/resources/rgg.html

Transcendent moments of change in the lives of women

CHERYL FISCHER & HEATHER WAITE

MOVING FROM FEAR TO COURAGE

Authors: Cheryl Fischer & Heather Waite

Publisher: Wildcat Canyon Press, 2001

Website: www.wildcatcanyon.com

Available in: Paperback, 224 pages. $13.95 (ISBN 1-885171-50-1)

Genre: Nonfiction/ Personal Triumph/Women's Issues

Summary

Many women have experienced a moment of transcendence — a moment in which her fear is overcome by one brief flash of insight, which she eventually recognizes as courage. The authors examine fear from a number of different viewpoints, exploring common (and often unconscious) fears than women feel, such as fear of success (or failure), intimacy, loneliness, aging, violence, or independence. They encourage readers to face and let go of those fears that stop them from achieving their potential. At the same time, they offer specific ways women can help themselves find solutions to problems, and ultimately make positive life choices.

Recommended by: *NAPRA Review*

"Inspiring and personal...with great respect and compassion...leaves the reader with a sense of genuine hope and enhanced empowerment."

Author Biographies

Cheryl Fischer has been a project coordinator for several child abuse organizations, and has also counseled at-risk families. She specializes in art therapy techniques. Fischer lives with her husband, Robert, in Marina Del Rey, California.

Heather Waite is a certified substance abuse counselor, whose volunteer work has included finding sober living environments for the homeless and chemically dependent, and working with people with schizophrenia. The author of *Calling California Home*, she lives in Pacific Palisades.

Topics to Consider

1) Do you think that women often see themselves as courageous?
    If not, why not?

2) Is there one person in the book who stands out to you as especially
    courageous? Why?

3) Is it a myth that women have a fear of success?

4) Is there a correlation between age and fear? Is it the same for men
    and women?

5) How are you dealing with the fears associated with the terrorist
    attacks of September 11th and subsequent warnings of attacks?

6) In the book, the authors define courage not as a static state, but as a
    transcendent moment in which someone acts *in spite of* their fear.
    Do you agree with that definition?

7) Is there a moment in which you transcended a fear that had
    previously kept you from acting? Why do you think it happened in
    that particular situation?

8) Do you think that gender has anything to do with an individual's
    response to fear?

9) Have you developed a way to discern what fear you will honor and
    what fear you will ignore?

MY MOTHER'S ISLAND

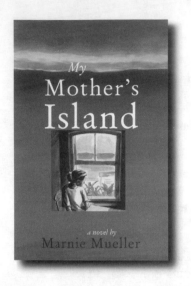

Author: Marnie Mueller

Publisher: Curbstone Press, 2002

Website: www.curbstone.org

Available in:
Hardcover, 238 pages. $24.95
(ISBN 1-880684-82-9)

Genre: Fiction/
Family/Personal Discovery

Summary

Sarah Elias arrives at her mother's modest bungalow in Puerto Rico consumed with worry that she won't be able to care for this woman from whose touch she recoils. She fears she won't even be able to cry at Reba's funeral and thus will reveal to the world the secret she's kept all her life, that she hates her mother. Sarah, who has always taken care of her mother's emotional needs, has steeled herself to single-handedly provide support to her mother as she dies, but gradually she allows people to help her through the ordeal. The story reaches its irrevocable conclusion in a death scene as cataclysmic as any in literature, and Sarah comes to terms with her mother and her past, finding at the end of her long journey both consolation and love.

Recommended by: Wally Lamb, author of *I Know This Much is True*

"My Mother's Island is a daughter's death watch: loving, angry, remorseful, and profoundly revealing of our lives as adult children."

Author Biography

Marnie Mueller was born in Tule Lake Japanese American Segregation Camp as described in her second novel, **The Climate of the Country**, which received rave reviews. Her award-winning first novel, **Green Fires: Assault on Eden,** was based on her Peace Corps experience. Mueller lives with her husband in New York City. Please visit her web site at *www. marniemueller.com.*

Topics to Consider

1) Sarah says she hates her mother. Is this a shocking thing to hear a daughter say? Should we believe that she really hates her, or are her feelings toward her mother more complicated than that?

2) Sarah doesn't have children, having chosen not to. Do you think her feelings for her mother would be different if she'd been a mother herself? Do you think she would have learned to be more tolerant of her mother's failings?

3) Sarah seems to love her father more than her mother. Do you think that the father's behavior got in the way of Sarah loving her mother and contributed to Reba's anger, or do you think that Sarah loved her father more intensely because of Reba's coldness and cruelty?

4) Do you think that the family's rootlessness contributed to the dysfunction in the family? Do you think the lack of religion and the mixed backgrounds of Sarah's parents contributed to the family problems and her loneliness as a child?

5) Even with all the difficulties Sarah has had with her mother, even though she feels damaged by her, she still makes the choice to care for Reba as she is dying. What do you think of such a choice? Would you be able to care for a parent you feel you don't love?

6) Sarah doesn't intervene in any way as her mother is dying. She doesn't bring her to the hospital and doesn't have an intravenous feeding tube put in when Reba can no longer keep food down. Do you think you could do this? Do you feel this was the right choice on Sarah's part?

7) The doctors and nurses in Puerto Rico encourage Sarah not to intervene, saying that this is the most merciful way to handle the situation. Does their position surprise you? Does their saying this seem to be culturally based? Would this have happened in mainland United States? Do you think it was a merciful choice, or should Sarah have tried to prolong Reba's life?

8) Do you think Reba was ready to die?

9) In the end, Sarah gives Lydia the house. Did you feel that Lydia earned the right to receive this gift?

AN OBEDIENT FATHER

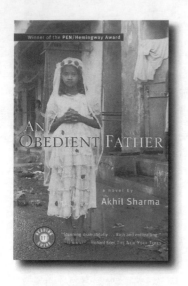

Author: Akhil Sharma

Publisher: Harcourt, 2001

Website: www.harcourtbooks.com

Available in:
Paperback, 288 pages. $13.00
(ISBN 0-15-60120-3)

Genre: Fiction/
Family/Personal Challenges

Summary

Ram Karan, a corrupt official in the New Delhi school system, lives in one of the city's slums with his widowed daughter and his little granddaughter. Bumbling, sad, ironic, Ram is also a man corroded by a terrible secret. With the assassination of the politician Rajiv Gandhi, Ram is plunged into a series of escalating and possibly deadly political betrayals. As he tries to save his family, his daughter reveals a crime he had hoped was long buried — and Ram, struggling to survive, must make amends after a life of deception. Taking the reader deep into a world of Indian families and politics, gangsters and movie stars, riots and morgues, *An Obedient Father* is an astonishing fiction debut, a work of rare sensibilities that presents a character as tormented, funny, and morally ambiguous as one of Dostoyevsky's antiheroes.

Recommended by: *The Nation*

"A stunning work that is both personal and political...perhaps the novel that, some might say, Arundhati Roy had wanted to write when she wrote **The God of Small Things.***"*

Author Biography

Akhil Sharma was born in India in 1971. His stories have been published in the *Best New American Stories* and *O. Henry Award* volumes, as well as the *Atlantic* and the *New Yorker*. He lives in Manhattan and works at an investment bank. This novel was a winner of the PEN/Hemingway Award and one of *USA Today's* Top 10 Books of the Year.

Topics to Consider

1) The novel opens with Ram Karan's statement, "I needed to force money from Father Joseph, and it made me nervous." How do this opening statement and the circumstances surrounding it help to establish the moral and ethical parameters of Ram Karan's world? What other early statements and episodes contribute to our sense of that world's moral disorder?

2) What is the role of politics in the lives of the characters? What parallels are established between personal behavior and morality, on the one hand, and political activity and ethics, on the other?

3) How do Anita, Ram, Asha, and other characters in the novel deal with the loneliness and other consequences "of being a person in the world"?

4) Misery, says Ram, "often makes me want to look away from the present and leads me to nostalgia." To what kinds of nostalgia does his "misery" lead him? Why might individuals in the India of Sharma's novel seek refuge in nostalgia, and with what success?

5) To what extent, and why, do Ram and others see the infliction of violence, cruelty, abuse, and brutality as impersonal misfortunes?

6) Why is admitting all his crimes to Anita and begging her forgiveness, in Ram's words, "the only way I could imagine any future"?

7) Why does Ram lose faith "in the power of confession," and what does he believe will be the rewards of confession? To what extent are his confessions genuine, and to what extent unreliable?

8) What kinds of corruption occur in the novel? What effects does corruption have on individuals, on families, on institutions and organizations, and on society itself?

9) What is the effect on Asha, herself, and others of Anita's unrelenting, unforgiving anger and fear? While determined to save her daughter from sexual abuse, what kinds of abuse does she herself inflict and cause to be inflicted?

THE PILOT'S WIFE

Author: Anita Shreve

Publisher: Back Bay Books, 1999

Website: www.twbookmark.com

Available in:
Paperback, 293 pages. $13.95
(ISBN 0-316-60195-0)

Genre: Fiction/
Relationships/Personal Challenges

Summary

Being married to a pilot has taught Kathryn Lyons to be ready for emergencies, but nothing has prepared her for the late-night knock on her door and the news of her husband's fatal crash. As Kathryn struggles through her grief, she is forced to confront disturbing rumors about the man she loved and the life that she took for granted. Torn between her impulse to protect her husband's memory and her desire to know the truth, Kathryn sets off to find out if she ever really knew the man who was her husband. In her determination to test the truth of her marriage, she faces shocking revelations about the secrets a man can keep and the actions a woman is willing to take.

Recommended by: *Newsday*

"From cover to rapidly reached cover, **The Pilot's Wife** *is beautifully plotted, tensely paced, and thoroughly absorbing."*

Author Biography

Anita Shreve is the author of the acclaimed novels *The Weight of Water, Resistance, Eden Close, Strange Fits of Passion,* and *Where or When.* Her award-winning short stories and nonfiction have appeared in the *New York Times Magazine, Cosmopolitan,* and *Esquire.* She lives in western Massachusetts.

Topics to Consider

1) The complex relationship between secrecy and intimacy is an important theme of ***The Pilot's Wife***. Consider the secrets kept by the following characters: Kathryn, Jack, Mattie, Robert, Muire. In each case, what motivates the deceiver? Who is protected and who is harmed by the secret? When, if ever, can deception be an expression of love?

2) Examine the conversation between Kathryn and Mattie (pp. 114-115), especially Mattie's question: "But how do you ever know that you know a person?" Is there a more satisfactory answer to this question than the one Kathryn offers?

3) Muire revealed the whole truth to Kathryn about Jack's secret life. How did this confession help Kathryn find the answers to her questions about how "real" her marriage was? Who is the "real wife?" (p. 265)

4) As a mother, is Kathryn obligated, at some future time, to share full knowledge of Jack with Mattie? Which parent do you think shared the stronger relationship with Mattie?

5) In what way was the house that Kathryn and Jack lived in for eleven years a metaphor for their relationship? Discuss the significance of Kathryn's discovery of the site of the Sisters' Chapel at the end of the book.

6) What devices does Shreve use to make her novel such a compelling read? Consider the flashbacks, the action, the style of language and word choice, and character painting.

For additional topics, see www.twbookmark.com

POPE JOAN

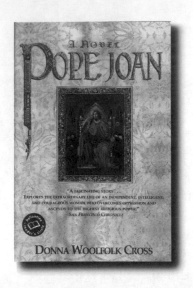

Author: Donna Woolfolk Cross

Publisher: Ballantine Books, 1997

Website: www.popejoan.com

Available in:
Paperback, 422 pages. $12.95
(ISBN 0-345-41626-0)

Genre: Fiction/
History/Inspiration & Faith

Summary

She is the legend that will not die — the woman who, disguised as a man, rose to rule Christianity in the ninth century as the one and only woman ever to sit on the throne of St. Peter. This international bestseller shares the dramatic story of this fascinating "Mystery of History" and provides a vivid record of what life was like during the Dark Ages. It has at its center an unforgettable woman, reminiscent of Jane Austen's Emma, Jean Auel's Ayla, and other heroines who struggle against restrictions their souls cannot accept.

Recommended by: *The Los Angeles Times*

*"It's so gratifying to read about those rare heroes whose strength of vision enables them to ignore the almost overpowering message of their own historical period...***Pope Joan** *has all the elements one wants in a historical drama — love, sex, violence, duplicity and long-buried secrets."*

Author Biography

Donna Woolfolk Cross worked for a publishing house in London before earning a master's degree in Literature and Writing from UCLA. The product of seven years of research and writing, **Pope Joan** is her first novel. Cross is at work on a new novel set in 17th century France.

Special offer: the author will chat online or by telephone with any reading group that selects *Pope Joan*. Interested groups should contact the author through **www.popejoan.com**.

Topics to Consider

1) How important is it that Pope Joan actually existed? Are there lessons to be learned from this story whether it's true or not? What are they?

2) Although the position of women in society has changed dramatically since the middle ages, do you feel there are similarities between the way women live in various societies today and the way they lived in society then?

3) Why did medieval society consider it unnatural and dangerous for women to be educated? What about the idea that learning impaired a woman's ability to bear children? What purpose might such beliefs have served?

4) Did Joan make the right choice at that moment when she decided to disguise herself as her dead brother? What would her life have been like had she chosen differently?

5) What happens to Joan when she tries to improve the lives of women and the poor? Why do you think Church and civic leaders were resistant to such improvements? Have there been similar instances in modern society?

6) What are the inner conflicts Joan faces? How do these conflicts affect the decisions she makes? Are they ever truly resolved?

7) Do you think Joan's secret would ever have been discovered had she not miscarried during the Papal procession or had she not become pregnant?

8) According to one reviewer, "Joan has the kind of vices — stubbornness and outspokenness, for example — that turn out to be virtues." Do you agree? If so, why? If not, why not?

9) If the Viking raid had not intervened to keep them apart, do you think Joan and Gerold could have had a happy life together? Why or why not?

10) What import, if any, does Joan's story have for the continuing debate over the idea of women priests? Does it support the idea, or argue against it?

QUEEN OF HARLEM

Author: Brian Keith Jackson

Publisher: Doubleday, 2002

Website: www.doubleday.com

Available in:
Hardcover, 272 pages. $22.95
(ISBN 0-385-50295-8)

Genre: Fiction/
Identity

Summary

Carmen England is a champagne-sipping, jet-setting social diva. She's not what Southerner Mason Randolph had envisioned when he trekked up to Harlem looking for an "authentic" black experience, but after just a few hours in her townhouse he finds himself under her spell, and questioning all he's ever believed about his place in the world. Mason sheds his preppie persona and emerges as "Malik," complete with a new vocabulary and a baggy wardrobe—his answer to taunts that he has spent his life as a "black boy blending." When he interviews to rent a room from Carmen, Mason realizes that masquerading as "Malik" will also win her sympathy, so he sets out to hide the details of his real roots (including his father's gold card and a promising future at law school). Things get even trickier when Mason meets his dream date, Columbia student Kyra, who brings his identity crisis full circle.

Author Biography

Brian Keith Jackson's other novels include *The View from Here*, which garnered the First Fiction Literary Award from the American Library Association's Black Caucus, and *Walking Through Mirrors*. Also the recipient of fellowships from Art Matters, the Jerome Foundation, and the Milay Colony for the Arts, Jackson lives in Harlem.

Topics to Consider

1) In what ways does Mason fear his talent and economic power? What does the final chapter tell us about Carmen's true fears?

2) How does the evolution of Harlem reflect the lives of its residents? What does the opening scene convey about Harlem's second Renaissance, especially compared to its first one in the early twentieth century?

3) Besides being the character who knows the truth about Mason, what does Jim's presence say about authenticity in general, particularly among whites who appropriate aspects of black culture?

4) When Mason steps off the number six train and receives his stinging introduction to Harlem from the real Malik, what keeps Mason from heading back downtown? What drives him to stay and invent a "ghettonian" version of himself?

5) How is Mason transformed by his mugging? What kind of turning point occurs during that scene, particularly when he orders his mugger to listen to the stolen CD?

6) Mason receives a lot of mothering. Compare the mothering styles of Joyce and Carmen. How do those two differ from Granny and her generation?

7) Though the chasm between rich and poor is a universal source of friction, why is this friction sometimes particularly intense in black America?

8) New York is often thought of as a city where it's possible to reinvent yourself an unlimited number of times. As Mason travels among several neighborhoods, and particularly when he is forced to walk a hundred blocks to get home, what does he observe about the many identities of New York itself?

9) Discuss some of the ways in which Mason's Harlem experience plays out in your town or neighborhood. When have you felt compelled to hide behind a false self? What are some of the daydreams that keep you going?

A Reading Group Companion is available at:
www.randomhouse.com/resources/rgg.html

QUIET TIME

Author: Stephanie Kane

Publisher: Bantam Dell, 2001

Website: www.writerkane.com

Available in:
Mass market paperback,
320 pages, $5.99
(ISBN 0-553-58174-0)

Genre: Fiction/
Family/Intrigue

Summary

What happens when a case goes cold and a murderer goes free? Sari Siegel finds out when Peggy Scott, a suburban wife and mother, is brutally slain on the eve of Sari's marriage to Peggy's college son Tim. More than the story of a girl coming of age against the backdrop of a brutal crime, *Quiet Time* is an exploration of moral responsibility in the context of a family in which duplicity and complicity are handed down from generation to generation.

Recommended by: Rikki Klieman, Court TV

"... Plunges deep beneath the surface of a fractured family relationship and a dysfunctional criminal justice system. Kane's work keeps your mind thinking and your heart racing – what a great read!"

Author Biography

Stephanie Kane grew up in Brooklyn, New York. She has practiced law for twenty years, first as a partner in the largest law firm in Colorado and then as a criminal defense attorney. She is also the author of *Blind Spot*. She lives in Denver with her husband, a federal judge.

> **Special offer:** The author will chat online or by telephone with any reading group that selects *Quiet Time*. Interested groups should contact the author at **www.writerkane.com**.

Topics to Consider

1) What role does "quiet time" play in the Scott family? Are there secrets in your family's past? Would they still be secrets today?

2) Sari Siegel and Peggy Scott each fled the place of her birth for a new life. Had Peggy lived, do you think she would ever have accepted Sari? What role do cultural and religious differences play in both women's marriages?

3) Sari takes irreversible steps to protect her future husband, Tim. What could Tim have done to alter the course of each character's fate? Knowing what Sari knew on the eve of her marriage, would you have gone through with it?

4) Money and passion are motives for murder. What pushes Peggy's killer over the edge? If a neighbor were found murdered, whom would you more readily suspect — an intruder or a family member? Is it easier for family members to "get away with murder"?

5) Blood is thicker than water. Should Tim have put Sari before his sister? Would the outcome have changed if Laura and Sari could have confided in each other?

6) Tim's Aunt Kay forces him to pay a terrible price for defending his mother's killer. Was that fair? Sari is also forced to choose between her husband and her personal values. At what point should family loyalty yield to one's own sense of justice?

7) Sari's father tells her to put Peggy's death behind her, and her mother says let the police handle it. Can closing your eyes ever have a positive outcome? What is the price of living a lie?

8) Why is the detective, Ray Burt, obsessed with the murder of Peggy Scott? How does his obsession create a bond with Sari? What needs of Sari's are fulfilled by Ray and his wife Marion?

9) How did the criminal justice system fail Peggy Scott? If you were on the jury, would you have voted to convict?

10) Kevin Day represents the "new breed" of cop. What makes him care about a cold case?

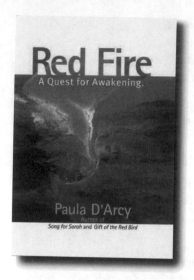

RED FIRE
A Quest for Awakening

Author: Paula D'Arcy

Publisher: Innisfree Press, 2001

Website: www.InnisfreePress.com

Available in:
Paperback, 128 pages, $ 13.95
(ISBN 1-880913-51-8)

Genre: Fiction/
Personal Discovery

Summary

In this elegant, simple, and inspiring fantasy, Paula D'Arcy reveals the journey of the soul from fear to love. For a young girl named Anastasia, born in the town of Status across the river from Quo, Nothing Ever Changes—until a Stranger arrives and awakens a great longing in her heart. This visitor enchants the children and tells them that a "Beautiful Being is hidden inside each part of life." As Anastasia becomes older, her memory of the Stranger dims until a tragic event causes her to question her life. Then she begins a quest to find this "fire that burns in the heart of all things."

Recommended by: Sue Monk Kidd, author of *When the Heart Waits*

"In the tradition of C. S. Lewis's **The Narnia Chronicles** *comes an enchanting and brave story from Paula D'Arcy, which opens us to the beauty and fire of spiritual awakening.* **Red Fire** *proves that sometimes fantasy is the best way to tell the truth."*

Author Biography

Paula D'Arcy is the author of ***Song for Sarah, When Your Friend is Grieving,*** and ***Gift of the Red Bird.*** As a therapist, she has ministered extensively to those facing grief and loss, drawing upon the personal loss of her own husband and child in 1975. Paula lives in the Texas Hill Country, and her time is spent writing and leading retreats and conferences.

Topics to Consider

1) Have you ever encountered the quiet "Presence" D'Arcy describes in the Prologue?

2) Have you ever experienced situations where questioning "what is" is dangerous or undesirable? How did this affect you? Have you bowed to "authority" even when it seemed contrary to intuition and intellect? Reflect on the way you resist making changes in your life.

3) Has a Stranger (in the form of a person or new idea) ever come into your life to reveal another way of being or call into question some of the beliefs you hold?

4) Part Two begins with a quote from Andre Gide which states that *"One does not discover new lands without consenting to lose sight of the shore for a very long time."* Have you ever experienced this kind of letting go?

5) In a book that was forbidden in the town, Anastasia read *"the greatest enemy of what you need to learn is what you believe you already know"* (page 59). Consider your own beliefs, patterns, habits that control your mind and may cloud your thinking.

6) While planting flowers one day, Anastasia had an "aha" experience as she felt the soil in her hands (page 60). What was her epiphany?

7) Anastasia felt she was on the right path and yet "nothing was happening" (page 65). Have you ever followed an inner urging and reached an impasse of waiting? What did you do?

8) Tenar the Magician asks Anastasia what she *really* wants (page 73). Why is that answer so important?

9) Anastasia talks about choosing safety (page 76). When have you made this choice? What did it cost? How might you begin to choose differently?

10) How have romantic dreams and visions shaped your life? What is your honest commitment or desire for change?

11) Toward the end of her journey, the Magician tells Anastasia, *"Love is always the way"* (page 107). What is your response to this statement?

SHADOW DANCING

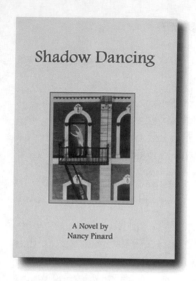

Author: Nancy Pinard

Publisher: Disc-Us Books, 2000

Website: www.nuvobookstore.com

Available in:
Paperback, 202 pages, $17.95
(ISBN: 1-58444-074-0)

Genre: Fiction/
Coming of Age

Summary

Emma Kate Thomas, a seventeen-year-old ballerina from a small midwestern conservatory, leaves her parents and partner behind when a world-famous director entices her to New York. But her imagined waltz to centerstage turns tango as soon as she arrives. Three male mentors vie to become her partner—each exacting his price—and she forges a family of immigrant women to prop her sagging spirit. As stagelight strikes, Emma Kate sees her shadow, recalls the defining moment of her childhood buried under the patchwork of her parents' love, and rediscovers the "dance" she learned in the heartland.

Recommended by: *The Boox Review*

"Pinard's introspective look at the power of childhood-instilled values and the depth of parental love is perfect for teen girls—and parents who may be doubting the worth of their side of the beautiful struggle."

Author Biography

Nancy Pinard danced with the Dayton Ballet Company and studied in New York at the studio of a national company. She now writes fiction and teaches creative writing at Sinclair Community College in Dayton, Ohio where she lives with her husband and two college-age sons.

Topics to Consider

1) Describe Emma Kate's childhood. What parts of her were nurtured? What parts neglected? What do you think of her parents' hiding the truth about Maura's death? What secrets did your family keep from you? How did learning the truth affect you?

2) Can you project what Emma Kate's life will be like from what you learn in the novel? How did the events of the novel prepare her for that life path? What events in your life paved the way for the person you became?

3) Emma Kate moves from a small pond to an ocean in chapter one. What insecurities does she feel? How does she offset those feelings? When have you made a similar growth step? How did you feel and how did you compensate?

4) What does Bobby teach Emma Kate about the process of making art? What are her goals? What are his goals for her? Who succeeds? How does the definition of success change over the course of the novel? How do you define success?

5) Why do Emma Kate and LeeLee become friends? How does diversity affect their relationship? Why do Porter and Donnelly become such an important part of their world?

6) Men play an important part in influencing Emma Kate's decisions. Name them and their various roles. What does Emma Kate gain and lose in each of those relationships? How do you feel about her treatment of each?

7) Note the irony in Emma Kate's decision to leave her father behind but put herself under the control of a man who renames her and prescribes her weight within a half pound. What ironic decisions have you made in your life? Why did you make them? Did those decisions foster or inhibit growth?

8) What "voices" from Emma Kate's past guide her in her decision-making? LeeLee's? Bobby's? What "voices" from your past do you still hear and how do they affect your decisions?

SHADOW OF THE HEGEMON

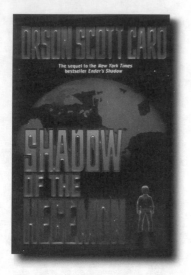

Author: Orson Scott Card

Publisher: TOR Books, 2001

Website: www.tor.com

Available in:
Hardcover, 365 pages. $25.95
(ISBN 0-312-87651-3)
Paperback, 464 pages. $6.99
(ISBN 812-56595-9)

Genre: Fiction/
Cultural & World Issues

Summary

Shadow of the Hegemon is the direct sequel to Orson Scott Card's international bestseller, *Ender's Shadow*. The Formic War is over, won by Ender Wiggin and his team of precociously brilliant child-warriors. The enemy is destroyed, the human race is saved. Ender himself refuses to return to the planet, but his crew has gone home to their families, scattered across the globe. But with the external threat gone, the Earth has become a battlefield once more. Nations wish to reassert their sovereignty. The children of the Battle School are more than heroes; they are potential weapons that can bring power to the countries that control them. One by one, all of Ender's Dragon Army are kidnapped. Only Bean escapes, and he turns for help to Ender's brother, Peter, who has already been manipulating the politics of Earth from behind the scenes. With Bean's help, he will eventually rule the world.

Recommended by: *Booklist*

"...so nicely integrated into the rest of the Ender canon that readers will be completely enthralled and left anxiously awaiting the next installment."

Author Biography

Orson Scott Card won both the Nebula and Hugo awards, the two most prestigious awards in the science fiction field, for two novels in a row, *Ender's Game* and *Speaker for the Dead*. While best known for his science fiction and fantasy works, he has also written ghost stories, nonfiction, plays and an historical novel. He lives in Greensboro, North Carolina with his wife and five children. Visit the author at *www.hatrack.com*.

Topics to Consider

1) In response to being captured, the children display the outwardly calm, strategic thinking that their Battle School training has inculcated in them. Does this represent their true emotions? How do these child soldiers cope with anger and fear?

2) Sister Carlotta tells Bean that she hopes he will someday have morality as well as intelligence. Is Bean an amoral character as the book begins? Is he any different by its end?

3) Bean discovers that because of his unique genetic makeup, he will live a life of unlimited abilities, but will die at an early age. Can a short, remarkable life ever take the place of a full life span?

4) Why are there so few girls and women in the worlds of the Battle School and the governmental and military leadership on Earth? Do men and women think, lead, or strategize differently?

5) Can the children make lives for themselves outside the context of the Battle School? Has their training and their war experience made it impossible for them to enjoy life on Earth? Once heroism is over, what gives life meaning?

6) Is Achilles a psychopath, or a willing conduit for evil? Where is the line between evil and madness? Could he have evolved any differently? What explains his power over others?

7) Is Bean arrogant, or vain? Is he realistic about his own abilities? Should people of enormous ability try to hide that ability, so as not to threaten those around them? Where is the line between confidence and self-aggrandizement?

8) How does this book treat questions of nationalism? Can human beings and nations ever transcend differences of religion, culture, or politics?

9) Is it ever appropriate to deny people bad news about their own fate in the interests of kindness or mercy? Are some truths too great for people to bear? Or is the freedom to make one's own fully informed choices paramount?

10) Was Petra right to preserve her own life? Is it ever right to sacrifice one innocent life in order to save millions of others?

11) What do gifted children — who often think and behave like adults — need from their parents?

TRANS-SISTER RADIO

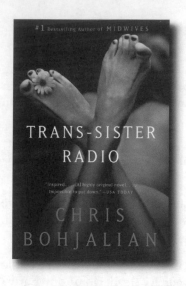

Author: **Chris Bohjalian**

Publisher: Vintage Books, 2001

Website: www.vintagebooks.com/read

Available in:
Paperback, 368 pages. $14.00
(ISBN 0-375-70517-1)

Genre: Fiction/
Identity/Relationships

Summary

When Allison Banks develops a crush on Dana Stevens, she knows that he will give her what she needs most: attention, gentleness, kindness, passion. But a few months into their relationship, Dana tells Allison his secret: he has always been certain that he is a woman born into the wrong skin, and soon he will have a sex-change operation. Allison, overwhelmed by the depth of her passion and unsure about her feelings, finds herself unable to leave Dana. By deciding to stay, she finds she must confront not only her own confused emotions but also the outrage of a small town community — hoping against hope that her love will transcend the physical.

Recommended by: *USA Today*

"Inspired ... A highly original novel ... Impossible to put down."

Author Biography

Chris Bohjalian is the author of seven novels, including *Midwives* (an Oprah's Book Club® Selection, *Publishers Weekly* Best Book and a New England Booksellers Association Discovery Title), *The Law of Similars*, and *Water Witches*. He lives in Vermont with his wife and daughter.

Topics to Consider

1) What stereotypes or common misconceptions about transsexuals does *Trans-Sister Radio* challenge? How is it able to reveal the reality beneath the stereotypes?

2) *Trans-Sister Radio* is alternately narrated by Carly, Will, Allison, and Dana. What effect does Bohjalian achieve by telling the story through four narrators rather than one? How do these differing perspectives shape and control our reactions to the story?

3) Does the novel seem to favor either Will's or Dana's point of view? Is it possible for chromosomes to make an "error"? Is there a "biological imperative" that determines gender? What ethical and social dilemmas arise with our increasing scientific ability to manipulate nature?

4) Why does a large part of the Bartlett community object to Allison living with a transsexual? Why do even liberal parents, who at least theoretically have no objection to gay marriage, draw the line at trans-sexualism? Are their fears understandable and justifiable? What are they based on?

5) In discussing transsexualism with her mother, Carly says, "we all want to cross over a lot more than we realize. We all want to be ... other" [p. 272]. Is she right? Why would we want to be something "other" than what we are?

6) How does Will go from being a person who regards Dana as "not normal" and sex-change surgery as a mutilation, to someone who not only accepts Dana but falls in love with her? What are the stages in this process? What moments draw him closer to Dana?

7) Looking back on their relationship, Allison feels she has been used by Dana. Is Allison right about Dana's motives? Has Dana deliberately deceived and manipulated her? Why doesn't he tell her of his plans at the beginning of their relationship?

8) When Glenn Frazier confronts Allison with the parents' concerns, Allison says, "Who lives with me is none of Richard Lessard's business." Glenn replies, "That's not true. You teach his daughter. He pays your salary" [p. 115]. To what extent do these opposing positions mask larger anxieties — about privacy, sexuality, education, morality — in America today?

AN UNFINISHED MARRIAGE

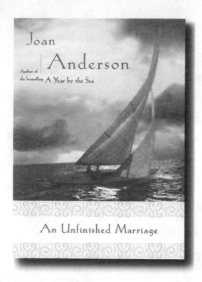

Author: Joan Anderson

Publisher: Broadway Books, 2002

Website: www.broadwaybooks.com

Available in:
Hardcover, 224 pages. $22.95
(ISBN 0-7679-0870-8)

Genre: Biography/
Personal Discovery/Relationships

Summary

When she first decided to take a year away from her husband, family, and friends, Joan Anderson's change of course was a courageous effort. Setting out against the tide of expectations, she learned from her inward retreat that a whole world was available to her beyond the duties of wife and mother that she had performed for years. In welcoming her husband, Robin, into her newly made sanctuary, she surprised her friends yet again. More importantly, she faced a new challenge in accepting the risk of balancing her needs with her husband's, of disrupting her carefully renewed sense of self. Through the twelve months of *An Unfinished Marriage*, Joan tested the waters of her family and her old friendships as well as her marriage and discovered that many of her relationships were still open to growth and change. As she looked at the people around her with new eyes, she saw something unexpected in them – a new image of her life as it was and how it could be.

Author Biography

Joan Anderson has written numerous children's novels as well as the critically acclaimed *A Year by the Sea* and *Breaking the TV Habit*. She is a frequent speaker on women's issues and the role of media in our lives, and holds "Weekend by the Sea" seminars. Anderson lives with her husband on Cape Cod.

Topics to Consider

1) Early in the book, Anderson refers to herself as a "recovering wife." What do you believe she is recovering from? In this case, how is her recovery as a wife related to her husband's transformation?

2) Anderson refers several times to the state of her marriage once the youthful "hormones" have worn off. Do you feel that there is a chemical or biological component that brings people together in their youth? Or is this shorthand for a different set of processes?

3) How do the financial changes a couple undergoes throughout a life-time change their larger relationship?

4) We are taught as adults that Prince Charming doesn't exist. But is there a kind of magic that brings people together? Romantic fantasy, like fairy tales and romance novels, is certainly seductive – but is it ultimately harmful or helpful?

5) What are the key components that Joan and Robin salvage and "recycle" that allow them to rebuild their marriage?

6) How can relationships with others be helpful in the process of redirecting a marriage?

7) Do you feel that the sharing of confidences is always beneficial? Are we more hurt by what we say or by what we keep quiet?

8) Do you think we need to repair ourselves before we can work on our relationships? Would Joan and Robin's reunion have been possible without their drastic separation?

9) Discuss the idea of rescue. Do you feel most often like the rescued or the rescuer? Do you expect someone to rescue you? Do you allow yourself to be rescued?

10) How do children, even adult children, affect a marriage?

11) How does the place we live define us? How great an impact do our surroundings have on us?

12) If you were to be isolated for two weeks, who would you choose to be with? How would it be to be alone with your spouse?

A WIDOW FOR ONE YEAR

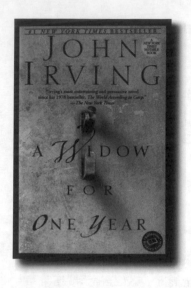

Author: John Irving

Publisher: Ballantine, 1999

Website: www.ballantinebooks.com/
BRC

Available in:
Paperback, 560 pages. $14.95
(ISBN 0-345-42471-9)

Genre: Fiction/
Personal Discovery/Relationships

Summary

Ruth Cole is a complex, often self-contradictory character—a "difficult" woman. By no means is she conventionally "nice," but she will never be forgotten. Ruth's story is told in three parts, each focusing on a crucial time in her life. When we first meet her—on Long Island, in the summer of 1958—Ruth is only four. The second window into Ruth's life opens in the fall of 1990, when Ruth is an unmarried woman whose personal life is not nearly as successful as her literary career. She distrusts her judgment in men, for good reason. *A Widow for One Year* closes in the autumn of 1995, when Ruth Cole is a forty-one-year-old widow and mother. She's about to fall in love for the first time. This is a multi-layered love story about the passage of time and the relentlessness of grief.

Recommended by: Barbara Kingsolver, *Washington Post Book World*

"… There's hardly a writer alive who can match [his] control of the omniscient point of view … Irving has written circles even around himself."

Author Biography

John Irving is the author of ten novels, among them *The Fourth Hand, The World According to Garp, The Cider House Rules,* and *A Prayer for Owen Meany.* He lives in Toronto and southern Vermont.

Topics to Consider

1) What role does imagination, lack of it, even fear of it, play in the lives and careers of the central characters?

2) What is the meaning and symbolism of the "feet" photo? Why do you think it became kind of a talisman for Ruth? What emotions does the photo evoke in you as a reader?

3) Discuss the life and writing career of Eddie O'Hare: his brilliance when being truly autobiographical, and his mediocrity when it came to believability in things that were "imagined".

4) How is Eddie, who appears as the most benign of characters, often the most powerful? How does he open the door to Ruth's future?

5) Discuss the idea that the books in Ruth's life and the characters in them were more fixed in Ruth's life than the flesh-and-blood people closest to her.

6) Why do you think Ruth decides to marry Allan? Why was he so safe? How was he different from her "type" of man — a type that disturbed her so?

7) Discuss the theme of humiliation in her novel-in-progress as well as Ruth's own unconscious quest for humiliation. Examine the themes of women, humiliation, and control.

8) Can matters of families, of love and hate (Ruth's father is the one she most loves and hates in her life), ever really be understood?

9) What changes occur in Ruth after she becomes a widow? How do these changes finally free her to fall in love at last?

10) What kind of emotions do you feel at the ending of the book? How have the characters of Ruth, Marion, and Eddie found, in essence, their way back?

THE WOODEN SEA

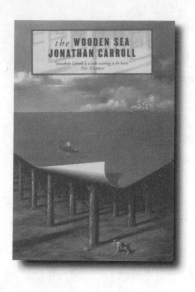

Author: **Jonathan Carroll**

Publisher: TOR Books, 2001

Website: www.tor.com

Available in:
Hardcover, 302 pages. $23.95
(ISBN 0-312-87823-0)
Paperback, 304 pages. $13.95
(ISBN 765-30013-3)

Genre: Fiction/
Humorous Touch/Personal Discovery

Summary

From the moment a three-legged dog limps into the comfortable life of Police Chief Frannie McCabe and drops dead at his feet, McCabe finds himself thrust into a new world of unaccountable miracles and disturbing wonders. The small town of Crane's View, New York, has long been a reassuringly familiar place for Frannie, a haven full of small comforts and domestic harmony, but now he finds himself afflicted by strange and inexplicable omens, such as a mysterious, multicolored feather that keeps insinuating itself into his past, present, and future, all of which now converge to throw Frannie's once ordinary life into doubt. Like it or not, Frannie has come face-to-face with the uncanny, and what he does over the next few days may have unforeseen consequences for the entire world.

Recommended by: Stephen King

"Jonathan Carroll is as scary as Hitchcock, when he isn't being as funny as Jim Carrey. If you've never read this wonderful fantasist, buy this book. You'll stay up all night and thank me in the morning."

Author Biography

A past winner of the World Fantasy Award, **Jonathan Carroll** is the author of several acclaimed novels, including ***The Land of Laughs***, ***The Marriage of Sticks***, ***Black Cocktail***, ***Bones of the Moon***, and ***Voice of Our Shadow***. His books have sold over a million copies worldwide. He lives in Vienna, Austria. Visit *www.jonathancarroll.com*.

Topics to Consider

1) One of the major themes is that of confronting one's perceptions: about life, about who we really are, and about what is "real." How have your own perceptions been challenged by this book?

2) Discuss what the author seems to be saying about the role of humanity in respect to the universe as a whole. Are we part of some inscrutable cosmic plan, or simply the butt of a vast cosmic joke?

3) Can both an adult and younger version of ourselves coexist at the same time? Is who we were the same as who we are now? Does time really pass, or is it merely our own perception of time that changes? If given the chance, would you want to see yourself as you once were? As you will become? Why or why not?

4) What effect does Frannie's experience with time travel have upon his view on his own life and that of his family, especially his father?

5) If you had a chance to visit with one of your own parents in the same time-adjusted manner as Frannie, what do you think you would see? What questions would you wish to ask them?

6) Frannie's friend George Dalemwood is described as "having no pre-conceived notions about anything." Is this a good philosphy for daily living? How might it be a negative?

7) About fear and love, Frannie says, "You create your fear. It's not out there like an infectious disease. Mostly it comes from love. When you love something so much that you can't bear to lose it, then fear's always nearby." Does loving someone or something so intensely make one weaker or stronger? What can be said about self-sacrifice as a gesture of love?

8) Discuss the idea of life as a random pattern of events. Are we doomed to re-live the mistakes of our lives until we get it "right"?

9) How does the story line square with the basic tenets and ideals of the world's major religions? Do you believe it was the author's intent to draw some parallels?

A Reading Group Guide is available with additional topics for discussion.

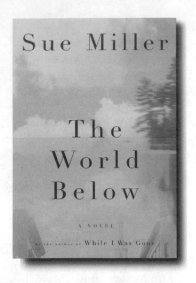

Author: Sue Miller

Publisher: Alfred A. Knopf, 2001

Website: www.aaknopf.com

Available in:
Hardcover, 275 pages. $25.00
(ISBN 0-375-41094-5)

Genre: Fiction/
Family/Personal Discovery

Summary

The World Below is a moving, often surprising exploration of the things people keep hidden from those closest to them. At its heart are two women, Catherine, a twice-divorced mother of three grown children who faces new possibilities and choices as she enters her fifties, and Georgia, Catherine's grandmother, the devoted wife of a country doctor who raised Catherine and her brother after the suicide of their mentally ill mother. As Catherine uncovers the world below the loving surface of her grandparents' life together, she comes to understand the impact of their secrets and of her mother's illness on the child she was and the woman she has become. Her discoveries transform her view not only of the past, but of her future.

Recommended by: *The New York Times*

"[Miller] has never written better about love and lust...Her work belongs at the top of the novel of domestic realism, of the relations between men and women, of hungry generations treading one another down but taking some pleasure in the interplay."

Author Biography

Sue Miller is the best-selling author of *While I Was Gone, The Distinguished Guest, For Love, Family Pictures, Inventing the Abbotts,* and *The Good Mother.* She lives in Cambridge, Massachusetts.

Topics to Consider

1) *The World Below* alternates between Catherine's voice and a third-person narrator. How does this approach help to define the two heroines and the times in which they live? How does it relate to Catherine's description of the way Georgia told her grandchildren about her life—"It was a little like the narrative voice of the Brothers Grimm or some of Rudyard Kipling's children's tales" [p. 13]?

2) Why does Catherine think that returning to her grandparents' house will help her resolve her feelings about Joe and their divorce [p. 18]? In what ways is her situation as a divorced woman parallel to her situation as an adolescent, when she came to live with her grandparents? Why does she begin her sojourn in the East by spending the night with an ex-lover [p.21]?

3) Georgia describes the sanatorium as "a place that existed outside of time" [p. 45]. What aspects of the patients' behavior strengthen this impression? What does the sanatorium provide that was missing from Georgia's life at home? Despite the rigid rules and daily routines, why does the atmosphere feel freer than the outside world? What specific rules of "ordinary" life are ignored or suspended at Bryce?

4) Why is Georgia attracted to Seward? To what extent are the qualities Georgia finds appealing attributable to his illness—and her own? Would she have fallen in love with him under other circumstances?

5) What are the lasting effects of Georgia's experiences in the sanatorium? How do they set her apart from her sister, Ada, and the other women in her community? Why does she consciously try to hide or suppress these differences? How does the society she lives in influence the choices she makes? Why does she begin to think of Seward as "someone she'd invented, a beautiful boy in a fairy tale" [p. 165]? What does her marriage to John represent in this context?

6) Why do you think Miller introduced Samuel, an older man, as Catherine's potential lover? In what ways does their relationship shed light on Catherine's marriages to Peter and Joe? What effect, if any, do you think age difference has on a marriage? How do the marriages in the novel support your position?

THE YEARS WITH LAURA DIAZ

Author: **Carlos Fuentes**

Publisher: Harcourt, 2001

Website: www.harcourtbooks.com

Available in:
Paperback, 530 pages. $14.00
(ISBN 0-15-600756-8)

Genre: Fiction/
Family/Personal Triumph

Summary

A radiant family saga set in a century of Mexican history, by one of the world's greatest writers. Carlos Fuentes's hope-filled new novel sees the twentieth century through the eyes of Laura Díaz, a woman who becomes as much a part of our history as of the Mexican history she observes and helps to create. Born in 1898, this extraordinary woman grows into a wife and mother, becomes the lover of great men, and, before her death in 1972, is celebrated as a politically committed artist. A complicated and alluring heroine, she lives a happy life despite the tragedies and losses she experiences, for she has borne witness to great changes in her country's life, and she has loved and understood with unflinching honesty.

Recommended by: *The Denver Post*

"Reading this magnificent novel is like standing beneath the dome of the Sistine Chapel...The breadth and enormity of Fuentes's accomplishment is breathtaking."

Author Biography

Carlos Fuentes was born in 1928. A diplomat who served as Mexico's ambassador to France, he has received many awards for his writing. The author of more then twenty books, including ***The Old Gringo*** and ***Terra Nostra***, he is recognized as one of the world's greatest living writers. He divides his time between Mexico City and London.

Topics to Consider

1) How does each kind of memory enumerated in the story play a role in the lives of the narrator, Laura Díaz, and others? What roles do memories play in all our lives?

2) How is the conflict between authoritarianism and tolerance played out in the various areas and phases of Laura Díaz's life? What other conflicts affect the lives of the characters? Which of these conflicts do you see at work in your life and the world today?

3) What is the relationship between power and money in the world of Laura Díaz? In what ways and to what degree, in Laura's world and ours, does "the rationale of power" have its way?

4) What is the impact on Laura Díaz of each death that occurs in her life? To what degree do you agree or disagree with Fuentes's claim, "We weep for the dead once and only once, and then we try to do what they could no longer do"?

5) In what ways do changing times and circumstances affect the role of women in Mexican society and the opportunities open to them? What might Fuentes want to say about the social, cultural, and religious/supernatural role of women?

6) What "ritual moments" acquire significance in Laura's life and in the lives of those close to her? How and why are those ritual moments important, and what lasting impact do they have? Why is ritual important in all our lives?

7) In what ways do Fuentes's characters, when the occasion arises, "respond to the challenge of heroism"? What kinds of heroism do the women and men of *The Years with Laura Díaz* display?

8) Jorge Maura asks, "Why do we believe and act in the name of our faith knowing full well we shall never be rewarded for the sacrifices faith imposes on us as a test?" How would you reply?

9) To what extent, if any, is Fuentes's novel an attempt to portray the "triumph of human freedom over God's tyranny"?

**Here are even more
great choices to consider ...**

What to Read Next
Picador USA

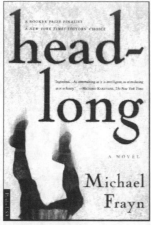

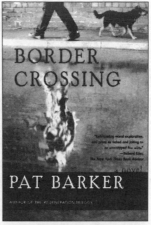

To discover what your reading group should be reading next, visit:
www.picadorusa.com

The Ballantine Reader's Circle is an esteemed collection of trade paperbacks, selected especially for reading groups. When you see the BRC logo on the outside, you'll find our reading group guide inside, complete with discussion questions and exclusive author interviews. From comfort fiction to historical novels, acclaimed literary works to penetrating nonfiction, you'll find the kinds of books that provide great reading and create lively discussions.

find yourself in... Milford-Haven

Locations to fuel your imagination, romances to stir your soul, friendships to warm your heart, issues to challenge your mind, and the mystery you'll want to solve

from acclaimed writer Mara Purl
... the Milford-Haven Novels
the compelling California coastal series
Based on the award-winning BBC radio drama

Milford-Haven, the little town with
global complexities and small town simplicities

"Mara Purl's mix of a soap-opera format is a smash hit in Britain."
– *the Los Angeles Times*
"In Mara Purl's books, the writing is crisp and clean, the dialogue realistic, the scenes well described. I salute her ingenuity."
– *Bob Johnson, Former Managing Editor, the Associated Press*
"Mara Purl tells stories from the heart. Don't miss her Milford-Haven series!"
– *Kathy (Mrs. Louis) L'Amour*

from Haven Books   www.havenbooks.net
10153 ½ Riverside Drive, North Hollywood, CA 91602 (818) 503-2518
Full Discussion Topics Lists at
http://www.havenbooks.net/fiction-readinggroupguides.shtml

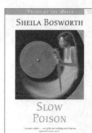

Ohioana Library Award Winner 2001

MAUDE (1883-1993):
She Grew Up with the Country

Author:　　Mardo Williams

Publisher:　Calliope Press, 1996

Genre:　　Nonfiction/biography

ISBN:　　　0-9649241-2-9　$22.95, Cloth

335 pages, 32-page photo insert

"Mardo Williams brings out the extraordinary in a seemingly ordinary century's worth of experiences in his fine biography of *Maude.*"—
Leonard Lopate, *NY & Co.*, National Public Radio

During her 110 years, Maude went from a 400-lb. wood-burning stove to a microwave oven, from an outdoor privy to indoor plumbing. She got the vote in 1920 and voted in the next 18 Presidential elections.

With poetry and human dramas (a suicide and two murders), written by a master journalist, the book shows the impact of the changing times on shy, unassuming Maude, her fun-loving husband Lee, and their four active children. They farmed 100 acres on the banks of Rush Creek in Logan County (Ohio).

** READING GROUPS—CONTACT CALLIOPE PRESS FOR 50% DISCOUNT (a paperback price of $11.47 for a hard cover book) **

Also available from Baker & Taylor, Ingram, Partners, & Partners West

Author Mardo Williams won an Ohioana Library Award in October 2001 (their first posthumous award) for his unique and outstanding lifelong literary contributions as an author and journalist. Williams began his writing career in 1927 as a reporter for the Kenton (Ohio) *News-Republican*, later joining the Columbus *Dispatch* as a daily columnist with byline. At age 88 he learned the computer and wrote this book as a tribute to his mother and other women like her at the turn of the century who did so much with so little—no electricity, no indoor plumbing. His children's book, ***Great-Grandpa Fussy and the Little Puckerdoodles***, was published May 2000. Before his death at age 95, he completed a novel, ***One Last Dance***, about a man in his 90s and and a woman in her 80s who fall in love. The book will be published in 2002.

Calliope Press, 400 W. 43rd St., #34B, NY, NY 10036; (212) 564-5068 (ph)
www.CalliopePress.com; e-mail: information@CalliopePress.com

RESOURCES

The Internet

Reading Group Choices Online — Includes a directory of over 575 guides available from publishers as well as more than 250 guides that can be printed directly from the site. **www.readinggroupchoices.com**

For new book information, reading lists, book news and literary events, visit **www.bookreporter.com, www.generousbooks.com, www.BookSpot.com,** and **www.BookMuse.com.**

Publisher Web Sites — Find additional topics for discussion, special offers for book groups, and other titles of interest.

Algonquin Books of Chapel Hill — *www.algonquin.com*

Back Bay Books — *www.twbookmark.com*

Ballantine Books — *www.randomhouse.com/BB/*

Broadway Books — *www.broadwaybooks.com*

Curbstone Press — *www.curbstone.org*

Doubleday Books — *www.doubleday.com*

HarperCollins — *www.harpercollins.com*

Henry Holt & Co. — *www.henryholt.com*

Knopf Books — *www.aaknopf.com*

Little, Brown & Co. — *twbookmark.com*

Penguin Putnam — *www.penguinputnam.com/guides/index.htm*

Picador — *www.picadorusa.com*

Random House — *www.randomhouse.com*

St. Martin's Press — *www.stmartins.com/rgg.htm*

Scribner/Simon & Schuster — *www.simonsays.com*

Vintage Books — *www.vintagebooks.com/read*

Warner Books — *twbookmark.com*

Newsletters and Book Lists

Book Club Today, an upbeat, innovative bimonthly publication for book club members and leaders. Issues contain book club profiles, national book club trends, reading group events and literary travel, themes for meetings, book reviews, and discussion questions. Annual subscription is $24.95 US (6 issues). Free sample issue upon request. Sponsor of "The Best Book Club in America" Contest. To enter the contest, or for more information:

info@bookclubtoday.com or
Book Club Today
PO Box 210165
Cleveland, OH 44121-7165
www.BookClubToday.com

Book Lovers Literary Magazine, quarterly book review publication with recommendations, book news, profiles of book groups, and more. Subscription: $10/yr. Contact:

booklove@execpc.com or
Book Lovers
PO Box 511396
Milwaukee, WI 53203-0241
(414)384-2300
www.execpc.com/~booklove

BookWomen: A Readers' Community for Those Who Love Women's Words, a bimonthly "bookletter" published by the Minnesota Women's Press. Includes recommendations, news about the book world, and articles for and about women readers and writers. Subscription: $24/yr. (6 issues). Contact:

books@womenspress.com or
Minnesota Women's Press
771 Raymond Ave.
St. Paul, MN 55114
(651) 646-3968
www.womenspress.com

Reverberations News Journal, Rachel Jacobsohn's publication of the Association of Book Group Readers and Leaders. Annual membership including subscription is $18. Contact:

ABGRL
Box 885
Highland Park, IL 60035
(847) 266-0431
E-mail: *rachelj@interaccess.com*

Literary Travel

Specialty World Travel. Annual trips with Diana Altman, Women's National Book Association member and travel consultant. Contact:

Diana Altman, President
Specialty World Travel, Inc.
128 Lowell Avenue
Newton, MA 02460
phone (800) 242-2346
E-mail: *info@specialtyworldtravel.com*

Books & Journals

Bibliotherapy: The Girl's Guide to Books for Every Phase of Our Lives by Nancy Peske and Beverly West. Published by DTP, ISBN 0-4405-0897-5, $13.95.

The Book Group Book: A Thoughtful Guide to Forming and Enjoying a Stimulating Book Discussion Group. Edited by Ellen Slezak and Margaret Eleanor Atwood. Published by Chicago Review Press, ISBN 1-5565-2412-9, $14.95.

Circles of Sisterhood: A Book Discussion Group Guide for Women of Color by Pat Neblett. Published by Writers & Readers, ISBN 0-8631-6245-2, $14.

Contemporary Multi-Ethnic Novels by Women Coming of Age Together in the New America by Rochelle Holt, Ph.D. Published by Thanks Be to Grandmother Winifred Foundation, $5 + s/h. Write to 15223 Coral Isle Ct., Ft. Myers, FL 33919.

The Go On Girl! Book Club Guide for Reading Groups: Works Worth Reading, Chats with Our Favorite Authors, by Monique Greenwood, Lynda Johnson and Tracy Mitchell-Brown. Published by Hyperion, ISBN 0-7868-8350-2, $14.95

Minnesota Women's Press Great Books. An annotated listing of 236 books by women authors chosen by over 3,000 women participating in Minnesota Women's Press Book Groups in the past 13 years. $10.95 + $2.00 s/h. (612) 646-3968.

The Mother-Daughter Book Club: How Ten Busy Mothers and Daughters Came Together to Talk, Laugh and Learn Through Their Love of Reading by Shireen Dodson and Teresa Barker. Published by HarperCollins, ISBN 0-0609-5242-3, $14.00.

The Readers' Choice: 200 Book Club Favorites by Victoria McMains. Published by Wm. Morrow, ISBN 0-6881-7435-3, $14.

The Reading Group Book: The Complete Guide to Starting and Sustaining a Reading Group by David Laskin and Holly Hughes. Published by Plume, ISBN 0-452-27201-7, $11.95.

The Reading Group Handbook: Everything You Need to Know to Start Your Own Book Club by Rachel W. Jacobsohn. Published by Hyperion, ISBN 0-7868-8324-3, $11.95.

Reading Group Journal: Notes in the Margin by Martha Burns and Alice Dillon. Published by Abbeville Press, ISBN 0-7892-0586-6, $16.95.

The Reading List: Contemporary Fiction, A Critical Guide to the Complete Works of 125 Authors. Edited by David Rubel. Published by Owl Books, ISBN 0-805055-27-4, $17.00.

Reading to Heal: A Reading Group Strategy for Better Health by Diane Dawber. Published by Quarry Press, ISBN 1-5508-2229-2, $10.95.

Talking About Books: A Step-by-Step Guide for Participating in a Book Discussion Group by Marcia Fineman. Published by Talking About Books, ISBN 0-9661-5670-6, $15.00.

What to Read: The Essential Guide for Reading Group Members and Other Book Lovers by Mickey Pearlman. Published by HarperCollins, ISBN 0-0609-5313-6, $14.00.

2002

	S	M	T	W	T	F	S

JANUARY
```
       1  2  3  4  5
 6  7  8  9 10 11 12
13 14 15 16 17 18 19
20 21 22 23 24 25 26
27 28 29 30 31
```

FEBRUARY
```
                1  2
 3  4  5  6  7  8  9
10 11 12 13 14 15 16
17 18 19 20 21 22 23
24 25 26 27 28
```

MARCH
```
                1  2
 3  4  5  6  7  8  9
10 11 12 13 14 15 16
17 18 19 20 21 22 23
24 25 26 27 28 29 30
31
```

APRIL
```
    1  2  3  4  5  6
 7  8  9 10 11 12 13
14 15 16 17 18 19 20
21 22 23 24 25 26 27
28 29 30
```

MAY
```
          1  2  3  4
 5  6  7  8  9 10 11
12 13 14 15 16 17 18
19 20 21 22 23 24 25
26 27 28 29 30 31
```

JUNE
```
                   1
 2  3  4  5  6  7  8
 9 10 11 12 13 14 15
16 17 18 19 20 21 22
23 24 25 26 27 28 29
30
```

JULY
```
    1  2  3  4  5  6
 7  8  9 10 11 12 13
14 15 16 17 18 19 20
21 22 23 24 25 26 27
28 29 30 31
```

AUGUST
```
             1  2  3
 4  5  6  7  8  9 10
11 12 13 14 15 16 17
18 19 20 21 22 23 24
25 26 27 28 29 30 31
```

SEPTEMBER
```
 1  2  3  4  5  6  7
 8  9 10 11 12 13 14
15 16 17 18 19 20 21
22 23 24 25 26 27 28
29 30
```

OCTOBER
```
       1  2  3  4  5
 6  7  8  9 10 11 12
13 14 15 16 17 18 19
20 21 22 23 24 25 26
27 28 29 30 31
```

NOVEMBER
```
                1  2
 3  4  5  6  7  8  9
10 11 12 13 14 15 16
17 18 19 20 21 22 23
24 25 26 27 28 29 30
```

DECEMBER
```
 1  2  3  4  5  6  7
 8  9 10 11 12 13 14
15 16 17 18 19 20 21
22 23 24 25 26 27 28
29 30 31
```

2003

JANUARY
```
          1  2  3  4
 5  6  7  8  9 10 11
12 13 14 15 16 17 18
19 20 21 22 23 24 25
26 27 28 29 30 31
```

FEBRUARY
```
                   1
 2  3  4  5  6  7  8
 9 10 11 12 13 14 15
16 17 18 19 20 21 22
23 24 25 26 27 28
```

MARCH
```
                   1
 2  3  4  5  6  7  8
 9 10 11 12 13 14 15
16 17 18 19 20 21 22
23 24 25 26 27 28 29
30 31
```

APRIL
```
       1  2  3  4  5
 6  7  8  9 10 11 12
13 14 15 16 17 18 19
20 21 22 23 24 25 26
27 28 29 30
```

MAY
```
             1  2  3
 4  5  6  7  8  9 10
11 12 13 14 15 16 17
18 19 20 21 22 23 24
25 26 27 28 29 30 31
```

JUNE
```
 1  2  3  4  5  6  7
 8  9 10 11 12 13 14
15 16 17 18 19 20 21
22 23 24 25 26 27 28
29 30
```

JULY
```
       1  2  3  4  5
 6  7  8  9 10 11 12
13 14 15 16 17 18 19
20 21 22 23 24 25 26
27 28 29 30 31
```

AUGUST
```
                1  2
 3  4  5  6  7  8  9
10 11 12 13 14 15 16
17 18 19 20 21 22 23
24 25 26 27 28 29 30
31
```

SEPTEMBER
```
    1  2  3  4  5  6
 7  8  9 10 11 12 13
14 15 16 17 18 19 20
21 22 23 24 25 26 27
28 29 30
```

OCTOBER
```
          1  2  3  4
 5  6  7  8  9 10 11
12 13 14 15 16 17 18
19 20 21 22 23 24 25
26 27 28 29 30 31
```

NOVEMBER
```
                   1
 2  3  4  5  6  7  8
 9 10 11 12 13 14 15
16 17 18 19 20 21 22
23 24 25 26 27 28 29
30
```

DECEMBER
```
    1  2  3  4  5  6
 7  8  9 10 11 12 13
14 15 16 17 18 19 20
21 22 23 24 25 26 27
28 29 30 31
```

READING GROUP CHOICES

BOOK GROUP MEETING DATES

January   _____

February   _____

March   _____

April   _____

May   _____

June   _____

July   _____

August   _____

September   _____

October   _____

November   _____

December   _____

January   _____

February   _____

March   _____

BOOK GROUP MEMBERS

Name _____

    Day phone _____ Eve. phone _____

Name _____

    Day phone _____ Eve. phone _____

Name _____

    Day phone _____ Eve. phone _____

Name _____

    Day phone _____ Eve. phone _____

Name _____

    Day phone _____ Eve. phone _____

Name _____

    Day phone _____ Eve. phone _____

Name _____

    Day phone _____ Eve. phone _____

Name _____

    Day phone _____ Eve. phone _____

Name _____

    Day phone _____ Eve. phone _____

Name _____

    Day phone _____ Eve. phone _____

Name _____

    Day phone _____ Eve. phone _____

7 Easy Steps for Leading Book Discussions

1. **Acknowledge your role as "facilitator" — not expert.**
   If it's your turn to lead the discussion, know that you are not expected to be an authority or expert on the chosen book. Your primary tasks are to open the discussion, keep it going, maintain a lively dialogue, and end the discussion on time. A great book discussion is the result of the thoughts and perceptions of a variety of different people.

2. **Select a book that is discussible.**
   Not all books are discussible. Look for topics that are controversial, writing that is interesting, authors who are complex beings, writing that will stir emotions or stimulate thought and prompt the reader to talk about what they've read.

3. **Tap available resources.**
   There are many sources for information. In addition to ***Reading Group Choices***, look online to *readinggroupchoices.com* and *bookreporter.com* for guides you can print directly from these web sites. Publishers also make reading groups available online. Check the resources pages in *Reading Group Choices* for a list. You don't need to research authors or develop discussion topics unless you want to. Guides are available for hundreds of books in print.

4. **Note your own response as you read.**
   Make notes as you read the book, highlighting or marking passages. What are your reactions, questions, or insights? Add the personal touch to your discussion. Share your thoughts during your discussion and invite others to comment.

5. **Lay some ground rules.**
   After you've introduced yourself to the group, remind members of the ways they can contribute to the discussion:
   a) Avoid "crosstalk" or talking over others.
   b) Be respectful. Keep an open mind.
   c) Try not to repeat what others have said. Speak up with something new or add to the previous comment.
   d) Acknowledge that there is no right or wrong, just differences of opinion.
   e) Be open to learn from others.
   f) If you are outgoing, be careful to allow space for others to share their thoughts.

6. **Call the question.**
   If you feel the group has begun to repeat itself, acknowledge your observation, ask for agreement if necessary, and pose a new topic.

7. **Balance the discussion.**
   Invite quiet members to share their thoughts. Watch for the introverts who have something to say, but are having a hard time getting in a word.

INDEX BY SUBJECT/INTEREST AREA

INDEX BY AUTHOR

INDEX BY AUTHOR

(continued)

INDEX BY AUTHOR
(continued)

INDEX BY GENRE

Nonfiction

Fiction

INDEX BY GENRE

Fiction (continued)

About *Reading Group Choices*

This publication, the 8th edition of ***Reading Group Choices,*** was developed and produced by Paz & Associates, whose mission is to join with publishers and bookstores to develop resources and skills that promote books and reading.

Books for potential inclusion are recommended by book group members, librarians, booksellers, literary agents, publicists, authors, and publishers. All submissions are then reviewed to ensure the "discussibility" of each title. Once a title is approved for inclusion, publishers are then asked to underwrite production costs, so that copies of ***Reading Group Choices*** can be distributed for the cost of shipping and handling alone.

Twenty thousand copies of ***Reading Group Choices*** are distributed annually to bookstores, libraries, and directly to book groups. Titles from previous issues are posted on our website at **www.** *readinggroupchoices.com.*

For additional copies of this publication, please call your local library or bookstore, or you may contact us by phone or email as shown below. We will be happy to ship copies to you directly, or let you know of a bookstore or library in your area that has obtained copies of ***Reading Group Choices.*** Quantities are limited.

For more information, please visit our website at:
www.readinggroupchoices.com

Or contact:

Paz & Associates

800/260-8605 — phone
dpaz@pazbookbiz.com — email

About Paz & Associates

The mission of Paz & Associates is to serve the bookselling community by empowering people and organizations with new skills and insights that significantly increase their ability to serve customers. We offer a variety of products and services to bookstores, publishers, and other book-related organizations, including the following:

- consulting with prospective and current retail booksellers on marketing, human resources, store design, merchandising, and business operations, including financial analysis, buying and inventory management

- *The Reader's Edge* bookstore newsletter marketing program

- *Opening a Bookstore: The Essential Planning Guide*

- *Opening a Bookstore: The Business Essentials*, 5-day intensive workshops (see web site for dates and locations)

- *The Training Guide to FrontLine Bookselling*

- Training Videos *Exceptional FrontLine Bookselling: It's All About Service,* and *Bookstore Merchandising Made Easy*

For more information, please visit our website at:
www.pazbookbiz.com

Or contact:

Paz & Associates

800/260-8605 — phone
dpaz@pazbookbiz.com — email

Reading Group Information
@ Your Fingertips

✓ Looking for other ideas about what to read?

✓ Want to know if a guide exists for a particular book?

✓ Need to print a guide in a hurry?

✓ Want title information from previous print editions of *Reading Group Choices*?

✓ Seeking guidance on how to start (and run) a book group?

✓ Want to order additional copies of *Reading Group Choices*?

For years, *Reading Group Choices* has been the #1 resource for book groups. Visit us online for full profiles on over 250 titles plus information on reading discussion guides that are currently available — from large publishers and independent presses. Reading Group Choices Online is an industry-wide, central resource.

What's New

Browse Guides by Subject

Search Available Guides

**Tips on Starting
A Book Group**

**Guidance for
Group Leaders**

Visit Reading Group Choices Online

www.readinggroupchoices.com